Agnes B...

ECONOMIC CLASSICS
EDITED BY W. J. ASHLEY

T. R. MALTHUS

ECONOMIC CLASSICS

Volumes now ready:

ADAM SMITH:
  Select Chapters and Passages

RICARDO:
  First Six Chapters

MALTHUS:
  *Parallel Chapters from the
  1st and 2nd Editions*

Forthcoming volumes:

  MUN
  CHILD
  TURGOT
  QUESNAI
  ROSCHER
  &c., &c.

PARALLEL CHAPTERS

from the

FIRST AND SECOND EDITIONS

of

AN ESSAY

on the

PRINCIPLE OF POPULATION

by

T. R. MALTHUS

1798 : 1803

New York
MACMILLAN AND CO.
AND LONDON
1895

Norwood Press
J. S. Cushing & Co. — Berwick & Smith
Norwood Mass. U.S.A.

Thomas Robert Malthus, the son of Daniel Malthus, a country gentleman living in Surrey, was born on Feb. 14, 1766. Entering Jesus College, Cambridge, in 1785, he was 9th Wrangler in the Mathematical Tripos in 1788; took Holy Orders; and in 1797 was elected to a Fellowship at his college. In 1805 he was appointed Professor of History and Political Economy at the East India College at Hailey-bury, a position which he retained until his death on Dec. 29, 1834. By his marriage in 1804 he had two daughters and a son.

His *Essay on the Principle of Population* arose out of discussions with his father, — who had been the executor of Rousseau, — over the opinions of William Godwin. In its first form, as published in 1798, it was a small loosely printed 8vo of 396 pp.: about one-third of it is here reprinted.

In its second form, as published in 1803, it was a 4to of 604 pp., containing about four times as much matter: about one-twentieth of it is here reprinted. The third edition appeared in 1806, the fourth in 1807, the fifth in 1817, the sixth in 1826. It was translated into German by Hege-wisch (1807), and into French by Prévost (1809, 2nd ed. 1852).

The other writings of Malthus were, *The High Price of Provisions* (1800), *Observations on the Corn Laws, Grounds of an Opinion on the Policy of restricting Importation, The Nature and Progress of Rent* (1814 and 1815), *Political*

Economy (1820), *Measure of Value* (1823), *Definitions in Political Economy* (1827), and *Summary View* (1830). In 1823 he contributed an article to the *Quarterly Review* on *Tooke*, and in 1824 another on *The New Political Economy;* and in 1824 he also wrote the article on *Population* in the *Supplement* to the *Encyclopædia Britannica*.

The chief authorities for his life are the biographical preface to the 2nd edition of his *Political Economy* (1836), by his friend, Bishop Otter, and the review of it by his colleague, Professor Empson, in the *Edinburgh Review* for January, 1837. The particulars thus derived have been supplemented from various sources in the biographical chapter of Mr. James Bonar's *Malthus and his Work* (1885).

The relation of the argument of the first edition of the *Essay* to that of the second has been the subject of comment by several writers, among whom may be mentioned Richard Jones (*Literary Remains*, 1859), Bagehot (*Economic Studies*, 1880), Mr. James Bonar (as above cited, and in *Philosophy and Political Economy*, 1893), Dr. J. K. Ingram (*History of Political Economy*, 1888, reprinted from *Encyclopædia Britannica* 1887), Professor Luigi Cossa (*Introduction to the Study of Political Economy*, 1893), and Mr. Edwin Cannan (*Theories of Production and Distribution*, 1893).

In reprinting the chapters from the first and second editions the original spelling and punctuation have been followed. After the second edition the text of the work remained substantially the same; but frequent changes of diction were made, in most cases to improve the style, but in some to remove objections by more carefully guarded statement.

AN

ESSAY

ON THE

PRINCIPLE OF POPULATION,

AS IT AFFECTS

THE FUTURE IMPROVEMENT OF SOCIETY.

WITH REMARKS

ON THE SPECULATIONS OF MR. GODWIN,

M. CONDORCET,

AND OTHER WRITERS.

LONDON:

PRINTED FOR J. JOHNSON, IN ST PAUL'S
CHURCH-YARD.

1798.

PREFACE.

—◦◆◦—

THE following Essay owes its origin to a conversation with
a friend, on the subject of Mr. Godwin's Essay, on avarice
and profusion, in his Enquirer. The discussion, started the
general question of the future improvement of society; and
the Author at first sat down with an intention of merely stat-
ing his thoughts to his friend, upon paper, in a clearer manner than he thought he could do, in conversation. But as
the subject opened upon him, some ideas occurred, which
he did not recollect to have met with before; and as he
conceived, that every, the least light, on a topic so generally
interesting, might be received with candour, he determined
to put his thoughts in a form for publication.

The Essay might, undoubtedly, have been rendered more
complete by a collection of a greater number of facts in the
elucidation of the general argument. But a long and almost
total interruption, from very particular business, joined to a
desire (perhaps imprudent) of not delaying the publication
much beyond the time that he originally proposed, prevented
the Author from giving to the subject an undivided attention.
He presumes, however, that the facts which he has adduced,
will be found, to form no inconsiderable evidence for the
truth of his opinion concerning the future improvement of

mankind. As the Author contemplates this opinion at present, little more appears to him to be necessary than a plain statement, in addition to the most cursory view of society, to establish it.

It is an obvious truth, which has been taken notice of by many writers, that population must always be kept down to the level of the means of subsistence ; but no writer, that the Author recollects, has inquired particularly into the means by which this level is effected : and it is a view of these means, which forms, to his mind, the strongest obstacle in the way to any very great future improvement of society. He hopes it will appear, that, in the discussion of this interesting subject, he is actuated solely by a love of truth ; and not by any prejudice against any particular set of men, or of opinions. He professes to have read some of the speculations on the future improvement of society, in a temper very different from a wish to find them visionary ; but he has not acquired that command over his understanding, which would enable him to believe what he wishes, without evidence, or to refuse his assent to what might be unpleasing, when accompanied with evidence.

The view which he has given of human life has a melancholy hue ; but he feels conscious, that he has drawn these dark tints, from a conviction that they are really in the picture ; and not from a jaundiced eye, or an inherent spleen of disposition. The theory of mind which he has sketched in the two last chapters, accounts to his own understanding, in a satisfactory manner, for the existence of most of the evils of life ; but whether it will have the same effect upon others, must be left to the judgment of his readers.

If he should succeed in drawing the attention of more able men, to what he conceives to be the principal difficulty in the way to the improvement of society, and should, in consequence, see this difficulty removed, even in theory, he will gladly retract his present opinions, and rejoice in a conviction of his error.

June 7, 1798.

CONTENTS.[1]

CHAP. I.

CHAP. II.

CHAP. III.

[1] The original tables of contents are given in order to display the character of the portions of the two Essays not reprinted.

CHAP. IV.

CHAP. V.

CHAP. VI.

CHAP. VII.

AN ESSAY ON THE PRINCIPLE OF POPULATION.

———◆———

CHAPTER I.

Question stated. — Little prospect of a determination of it, from the enmity of the opposing parties. — The principal argument against the perfectibility of man and of society has never been fairly answered. — Nature of the difficulty arising from population. — Outline of the principal argument of the essay.

THE great and unlooked for discoveries that have taken place of late years in natural philosophy; the increasing diffusion of general knowledge from the extension of the art of printing; the ardent and unshackled spirit of inquiry that prevails throughout the lettered, and even unlettered world; the new and extraordinary lights that have been thrown on political subjects, which dazzle and astonish the understanding; and particularly that tremendous phenomenon in the political horizon the French Revolution, which, like a blazing comet, seems destined either to inspire with fresh life and vigour, or to scorch up and destroy the thinking inhabitants of the earth, have all concurred to lead able men into the opinion, that we were touching upon a period big with the most important changes, changes that would in some measure be decisive of the future fate of mankind.

It has been said, that the great question is now at issue, whether man shall henceforth start forwards with accelerated velocity towards illimitable, and hitherto unconceived improvement; or be condemned to a perpetual oscillation between happiness and misery, and after every effort remain still at an immeasurable distance from the wished-for goal.

Yet, anxiously as every friend of mankind must look forwards to the termination of this painful suspense; and, eagerly as the inquiring mind would hail every ray of light that might assist its view into futurity, it is much to be lamented, that the writers on each side of this momentous question still keep far aloof from each other. Their mutual arguments do not meet with a candid examination. The question is not brought to rest on fewer points; and even in theory scarcely seems to be approaching to a decision.

The advocate for the present order of things, is apt to treat the sect of speculative philosophers, either as a set of artful and designing knaves, who preach up ardent benevolence, and draw captivating pictures of a happier state of society, only the better to enable them to destroy the present establishments, and to forward their own deep-laid schemes of ambition: or, as wild and mad-headed enthusiasts, whose silly speculations, and absurd paradoxes, are not worthy the attention of any reasonable man.

The advocate for the perfectibility of man, and of society, retorts on the defender of establishments a more than equal contempt. He brands him as the slave of the most miserable, and narrow prejudices; or, as the defender of the abuses of civil society, only because he profits by them. He paints him either as a character who prostitutes his understanding to his interest; or as one whose powers of mind are not of a size to grasp anything great and noble; who cannot see above five yards before him; and who must therefore be utterly unable to take in the views of the enlightened benefactor of mankind.

In this unamicable contest, the cause of truth cannot but suffer. The really good arguments on each side of the question are not allowed to have their proper weight. Each pursues his own theory, little solicitous to correct, or improve it, by an attention to what is advanced by his opponents.

The friend of the present order of things condemns all political speculations in the gross. He will not even condescend to examine the grounds from which the perfectibility of society is inferred. Much less will he give himself the trouble in a fair and candid manner to attempt an exposition of their fallacy.

The speculative philosopher equally offends against the cause of truth. With eyes fixed on a happier state of society, the blessings of which he paints in the most captivating colours, he allows himself to indulge in the most bitter invectives against every present establishment, without applying his talents to consider the best and safest means of removing abuses, and without seeming to be aware of the tremendous obstacles that threaten, even in theory, to oppose the progress of man towards perfection.

It is an acknowledged truth in philosophy, that a just theory will always be confirmed by experiment. Yet so much friction, and so many minute circumstances occur in practice, which it is next to impossible for the most enlarged and penetrating mind to foresee, that on few subjects can any theory be pronounced just, that has not stood the test of experience. But an untried theory cannot be advanced as probable, much less as just, till all the arguments against it have been maturely weighed, and clearly and consistently confuted.

I have read some of the speculations on the perfectibility of man and of society with great pleasure. I have been warmed and delighted with the enchanting picture which they hold forth. I ardently wish for such happy improvements. But I see great, and, to my understanding, unconquerable difficulties in the way to them. These difficulties it is my present purpose to state ; declaring, at the same time, that so far from exulting in them, as a cause of triumphing over the friends of innovation, nothing would give me greater pleasure than to see them completely removed.

The most important argument that I shall adduce is certainly not new. The principles on which it depends have been explained in part by Hume, and more at large by Dr. Adam Smith. It has been advanced and applied to the present subject, though not with its proper weight, or in the most forcible point of view, by Mr. Wallace : and it may probably have been stated by many writers that I have never met with. I should certainly, therefore, not think of advancing it again, though I mean to place it in a point of view in some degree different from any that I have hitherto seen, if it had ever been fairly and satisfactorily answered.

The cause of this neglect on the part of the advocates for the perfectibility of mankind is not easily accounted for. I cannot doubt the talents of such men as Godwin and Condorcet. I am unwilling to doubt their candour. To my understanding, and probably to that of most others, the difficulty appears insurmountable. Yet these men of acknowledged ability and penetration, scarcely deign to notice it, and hold on their course in such speculations, with unabated ardour and undiminished confidence. I have certainly no right to say that they purposely shut their eyes to such arguments. I ought rather to doubt the validity of them, when neglected by such men, however forcibly their truth may strike my own mind. Yet in this respect it must be acknowledged that we are all of us too prone to err. If I saw a glass of wine repeatedly presented to a man, and he took no notice of it, I should be apt to think that he was blind or uncivil. A juster philosophy might teach me rather to think that my eyes deceived me, and that the offer was not really what I conceived it to be.

In entering upon the argument I must premise that I put out of the question, at present, all mere conjectures ; that is, all suppositions, the probable realization of which cannot be inferred upon any just philosophical grounds. A writer may tell me that he thinks man will ultimately become an ostrich. I cannot properly contradict him. But before he can expect to bring any reasonable person over to his opinion, he ought to show that the necks of mankind have been gradually elongating ; that the lips have grown harder, and more prominent ; that the legs and feet are daily altering their shape ; and that the hair is beginning to change into stubs of feathers. And till the probability of so wonderful a conversion can be shown, it is surely lost time and lost eloquence to expatiate on the happiness of man in such a state ; to describe his powers, both of running and flying ; to paint him in a condition where all narrow luxuries would be contemned ; where he would be employed only in collecting the necessaries of life; and where, consequently, each man's share of labour would be light, and his portion of leisure ample.

I think I may fairly make two postulata.

First, That food is necessary to the existence of man.

Secondly, That the passion between the sexes is necessary, and will remain nearly in its present state.

These two laws ever since we have had any knowledge of mankind, appear to have been fixed laws of our nature; and, as we have not hitherto seen any alteration in them, we have no right to conclude that they will ever cease to be what they are now, without an immediate act of power in that Being who first arranged the system of the universe; and for the advantage of his creatures, still executes, according to fixed laws, all its various operations.

I do not know that any writer has supposed that on this earth man will ultimately be able to live without food. But Mr. Godwin has conjectured that the passion between the sexes may in time be extinguished. As, however, he calls this part of his work, a deviation into the land of conjecture, I will not dwell longer upon it at present, than to say, that the best arguments for the perfectibility of man are drawn from a contemplation of the great progress that he has already made from the savage state, and the difficulty of saying where he is to stop. But towards the extinction of the passion between the sexes, no progress whatever has hitherto been made. It appears to exist in as much force at present as it did two thousand, or four thousand years ago. There are individual exceptions now as there always have been. But, as these exceptions do not appear to increase in number, it would surely be a very unphilosophical mode of arguing, to infer merely from the existence of an exception, that the exception would, in time, become the rule, and the rule the exception.

Assuming, then, my postulata as granted, I say, that the power of population is indefinitely greater than the power in the earth to produce subsistence for man.

Population, when unchecked, increases in a geometrical ratio. Subsistence only increases in an arithmetical ratio. A slight acquaintance with numbers will show the immensity of the first power in comparison of the second.

By that law of our nature which makes food necessary to the life of man, the effects of these two unequal powers must be kept equal.

This implies a strong and constantly operating check on population from the difficulty of subsistence. This difficulty must fall some where ; and must necessarily be severely felt by a large portion of mankind.

Through the animal and vegetable kingdoms, nature has scattered the seeds of life abroad with the most profuse and liberal hand. She has been comparatively sparing in the room, and the nourishment necessary to rear them. The germs of existence contained in this spot of earth, with ample food, and ample room to expand it, would fill millions of worlds in the course of a few thousand years. Necessity, that imperious, all-pervading law of nature, restrains them within the prescribed bounds. The race of plants, and the race of animals shrink under this great restrictive law. And the race of man cannot, by any efforts of reason, escape from it. Among plants and animals its effects are waste of seed, sickness, and premature death. Among mankind, misery and vice. The former, misery, is an absolutely necessary consequence of it. Vice is a highly probable consequence, and we therefore see it abundantly prevail; but it ought not, perhaps, to be called an absolutely necessary consequence. The ordeal of virtue is to resist all temptation to evil.

This natural inequality of the two powers of population, and of production in the earth, and that great law of our nature which must constantly keep their effects equal, form the great difficulty that to me appears insurmountable in the way to perfectibility of society. All other arguments are of slight and subordinate consideration in comparison of this. I see no way by which man can escape from the weight of this law which pervades all animated nature. No fancied equality, no agrarian regulations in their utmost extent, could remove the pressure of it even for a single century. And it appears, therefore, to be decisive against the possible existence of a society, all the members of which should live in ease, happiness, and comparative leisure; and feel no anxiety about providing the means of subsistence for themselves and families.

Consequently, if the premises are just, the argument is conclusive against the perfectibility of the mass of mankind.

I have thus sketched the general outline of the argument; but I will examine it more particularly; and I think it will be found that experience, the true source and foundation of all knowledge, invariably confirms its truth.

CHAPTER II.

I SAID that population, when unchecked, increased in a geometrical ratio; and subsistence for man in an arithmetical ratio.

Let us examine whether this proposition be just.

I think it will be allowed, that no state has hitherto existed (at least that we have any account of) where the manners were so pure and simple, and the means of subsistence so abundant, that no check whatever has existed to early marriages; among the lower classes, from a fear of not providing well for their families; or among the higher classes, from a fear of lowering their condition in life. Consequently in no state that we have yet known, has the power of population been left to exert itself with perfect freedom.

Whether the law of marriage be instituted or not, the dictate of nature and virtue, seems to be an early attachment to one woman. Supposing the liberty of changing in the case of an unfortunate choice, this liberty would not affect population till it arose to a height greatly vicious ; and we are now supposing the existence of a society where vice is scarcely known.

In a state therefore of great equality and virtue, where pure and simple manners prevailed, and where the means of subsistence were so abundant, that no part of the society could have any fears about providing amply for a family, the power of population being left to exert itself unchecked, the increase of the human species would evidently be much greater than any increase that has been hitherto known.

In the United States of America, where the means of subsistence have been more ample, the manners of the people more pure, and consequently the checks to early marriages fewer, than in any of the modern states of Europe, the population has been found to double itself in twenty-five years.

This ratio of increase, though short of the utmost power of population, yet as the result of actual experience, we will take as our rule ; and say,

That population, when unchecked, goes on doubling itself every twenty-five years, or increases in a geometrical ratio.

Let us now take any spot of earth, this Island for instance, and see in what ratio the subsistence it affords can be supposed to increase. We will begin with it under its present state of cultivation.

If I allow that by the best possible policy, by breaking up more land, and by great encouragements to agriculture, the produce of this Island may be doubled in the first twenty-five years, I think it will be allowing as much as any person can well demand.

In the next twenty-five years, it is impossible to suppose that the produce could be quadrupled. It would be contrary to all our knowledge of the qualities of land. The very utmost that we can conceive, is, that the increase in the second twenty-five years might equal the present produce. Let us then take this for our rule, though certainly far beyond the truth ; and allow that by great exertion, the whole produce of the Island might be increased every twenty-five years, by a quantity of subsistence equal to what it at present produces. The most enthusiastic speculator cannot suppose a greater increase than this. In a few centuries it would make every acre of land in the Island like a garden.

Yet this ratio of increase is evidently arithmetical.

It may be fairly said, therefore, that the means of subsistence increase in an arithmetical ratio.

Let us now bring the effects of these two ratios together. The population of the Island is computed to be about seven millions ; and we will suppose the present produce equal to the support of such a number. In the first twenty-five years the population would be fourteen millions ; and the food being also doubled, the means of subsistence would be equal to this increase. In the next twenty-five years the population would be twenty-eight millions ; and the means of subsistence only equal to the support of twenty-one millions. In the next period, the population would be fifty-six millions, and the means of subsistence just sufficient for half that number. And at the conclusion of the first century, the population would be one hundred and twelve millions, and the means of subsistence only equal to the support of thirty-five millions ; which would leave a population of seventy-seven millions totally unprovided for.

A great emigration necessarily implies unhappiness of some kind or other in the country that is deserted. For few persons will leave their families, connections, friends, and native land, to seek a settlement in untried foreign climes, without some strong subsisting causes of uneasiness where they are, or the hope of some great advantages in the place to which they are going.

But to make the argument more general, and less interrupted by the partial views of emigration, let us take the whole earth, instead of one spot, and suppose that the restraints to population were universally removed. If the subsistence for man that the earth affords was to be increased every twenty-five years by a quantity equal to what the whole world at present produces, this would allow the power of production in the earth to be absolutely unlimited, and its ratio of increase much greater than we can conceive that any possible exertions of mankind could make it.

Taking the population of the world at any number, a thousand millions, for instance, the human species would increase in the ratio of — 1, 2, 4, 8, 16, 32, 64, 128, 256, 512, etc., and subsistence as — 1, 2, 3, 4, 5, 6, 7, 8, 9, 10, etc. In two centuries and a quarter the population would be to the means of subsistence as 512 to 10 ; in three centuries, as 4096 to 13 ; and in two thousand years the difference would be almost incalculable, though the produce in that time would have increased to an immense extent.

No limits whatever are placed to the productions of the earth ; they may increase forever and be greater than any assignable quantity ; yet still the power of population being a power of superior order, the increase of the human species can only be kept commensurate to the increase of the means of subsistence, by the constant operation of the strong law of necessity acting as a check upon the greater power.

The effects of this check remain now to be considered.

Among plants and animals the view of the subject is simple. They are all impelled by a powerful instinct to the increase of their species; and this instinct is interrupted by no reasoning, or doubts about providing for their offspring. Wherever therefore there is liberty, the power of increase is exerted; and the superabundant effects are repressed afterwards by want of room and nourishment, which is common to animals and plants; and among animals, by becoming the prey of others.

The effects of this check on man are more complicated.

Impelled to the increase of his species by an equally powerful instinct, reason interrupts his career, and asks him whether he may not bring beings into the world, for whom he cannot provide the means of subsistence. In a state of equality, this would be the simple question. In the present state of society, other considerations occur. Will he not lower his rank in life? Will he not subject himself to greater difficulties than he at present feels? Will he not be obliged to labour harder? and if he has a large family, will his utmost exertions enable him to support them? May he not see his offspring in rags and misery, and clamouring for bread that he cannot give them? And may he not be reduced to the grating necessity of forfeiting his independence, and of being obliged to the sparing hand of charity for support?

These considerations are calculated to prevent, and cer-

tainly do prevent, a very great number in all civilized nations
from pursuing the dictate of nature in an early attachment
to one woman. And this restraint almost necessarily, though
not absolutely so, produces vice. Yet in all societies, even
those that are most vicious, the tendency to a virtuous attachment is so strong, that there is a constant effort towards an
increase of population. This constant effort as constantly
tends to subject the lower classes of the society to distress,
and to prevent any great permanent amelioration of their
condition.

The way in which these effects are produced seems to be
this.

We will suppose the means of subsistence in any country
just equal to the easy support of its inhabitants. The
constant effort towards population, which is found to act
even in the most vicious societies, increases the number
of people before the means of subsistence are increased.
The food therefore which before supported seven millions,
must now be divided among seven millions and a half, or
eight millions. The poor consequently must live much
worse, and many of them be reduced to severe distress.
The number of labourers also being above the proportion
of the work in the market, the price of labour must tend
toward a decrease; while the price of provisions would at
the same time tend to rise. The labourer therefore must
work harder to earn the same as he did before. During
this season of distress, the discouragements to marriage, and
the difficulty of rearing a family are so great, that population
is at a stand. In the meantime the cheapness of labour,
the plenty of labourers, and the necessity of an increased

industry amongst them, encourage cultivators to employ more labour upon their land; to turn up fresh soil, and to manure and improve more completely what is already in tillage; till ultimately the means of subsistence become in the same proportion to the population as at the period from which we set out. The situation of the labourer being then again tolerably comfortable, the restraints to population are in some degree loosened; and the same retrograde and progressive movements with respect to happiness are repeated.

This sort of oscillation will not be remarked by superficial observers; and it may be difficult even for the most penetrating mind to calculate its periods. Yet that in all old states some such vibration does exist; though from various transverse causes, in a much less marked, and in a much more irregular manner than I have described it, no reflecting man who considers the subject deeply can well doubt.

Many reasons occur why this oscillation has been less obvious, and less decidedly confirmed by experience, than might naturally be expected.

One principal reason is, that the histories of mankind that we possess are histories only of the higher classes. We have but few accounts that can be depended upon of the manners and customs of that part of mankind, where these retrograde and progressive movements chiefly take place. A satisfactory history of this kind, of one people, and of one period, would require the constant and minute attention of an observing mind during a long life. Some of the objects of inquiry would be, in what proportion to the number of adults was the number of marriages: to what extent vicious customs prevailed in consequence of the restraints upon matrimony : what was the comparative mortality among the children of the most distressed part of the community, and those who lived rather more at their ease : what were the variations in the real price of labour : and what were the observable differences in the state of the lower classes of society, with respect to ease and happiness, at different times during a certain period.

Such a history would tend greatly to elucidate the manner in which the constant check upon population acts ; and would probably prove the existence of the retrograde and progressive movements that have been mentioned ; though the times of their vibration must necessarily be rendered irregular, from the operation of many interrupting causes such as, the introduction or failure of certain manufact ures : a greater or less prevalent spirit of agricultural enterprise : years of plenty, or years of scarcity : wars and pestilence : poor laws : the invention of processes for shorten ing labour without the proportional extension of the market for the commodity : and, particularly, the difference between the nominal and real price of labour ; a circumstance which has perhaps more than any other contributed to conceal this oscillation from common view.

It very rarely happens that the nominal price of labour universally falls : but we well know that it frequently remains the same, while the nominal price of provisions has been gradually increasing. This is, in effect, a real fall in the price of labour ; and during this period, the condition of the lower orders of the community must gradually grow worse and worse. But the farmers and capitalists are growing rich from the real cheapness of labour. Their increased capital enable them to employ a greater number of men. Work, therefore, may be plentiful; and the price of labour would consequently rise. But the want of freedom in the market of labour, which occurs more or less in all communities, either from parish laws, or the more general cause of the facility of combination among the rich, and its difficulty among the poor, operates to prevent the price of labour from rising at the natural period, and keeps it down some time longer; perhaps till a year of scarcity, when the clamour is too loud, and the necessity too apparent to be resisted.

The true cause of the advance in the price of labour is thus concealed; and the rich affect to grant it as an act of compassion and favour to the poor, in consideration of a year of scarcity; and when plenty returns, indulge themselves in the most unreasonable of all complaints, that the price does not again fall; when a little reflection would shew them that it must have risen long before, but from an unjust conspiracy of their own.

But though the rich by unfair combinations, contribute frequently to prolong a season of distress among the poor; yet no possible form of society could prevent the almost constant action of misery upon a great part of mankind, if in a state of inequality, and upon all, if all were equal.

The theory on which the truth of this position depends appears to me so extremely clear, that I feel at a loss to conjecture what part of it can be denied.

That population cannot increase without the means of subsistence, is a proposition so evident that it needs no illustration.

That population does invariably increase where there are

c

the means of subsistence, the history of every people that have ever existed will abundantly prove.

And, that the superior power of population cannot be checked without producing misery or vice, the ample portion of these two bitter ingredients in the cup of human life, and the continuance of the physical causes that seem to have produced them, bear too convincing a testimony.

But in order more fully to ascertain the validity of these three propositions, let us examine the different states in which mankind have been known to exist. Even a cursory view will, I think, be sufficient to convince us that these propositions are incontrovertible truths.

CHAPTER IV.

. . . Slow increase of population at present in most of the states of Europe. — The two principal checks to population. — The first or preventive check examined with regard to England.

. . . In examining the principal states of modern Europe, we shall find, that though they have increased very considerably in population since they were nations of shepherds, yet that, at present, their progress is but slow ; and instead of doubling their numbers every twenty-five years, they require three or four hundred years, or more, for that purpose. Some, indeed, may be absolutely stationary, and others even retrograde. The cause of this slow progress in population cannot be traced to a decay of the passion between the sexes. We have sufficient reason to think that this natural propensity exists still in undiminished vigour. Why then do not its effects appear in a rapid increase of the human species? An intimate view of the state of society in any one country in Europe, which may serve equally for all, will enable us to answer this question, and to say, that a foresight of the difficulties attending the rearing of a family, acts as a preventive check ; and the actual distress of some of the lower classes, by which they are disabled from giving the proper food and attention to their children, acts as a positive check, to the natural increase of population.

England, as one of the most flourishing states of Europe, may be fairly taken for an example, and the observations made, will apply with but little variation to any other country where the population increases slowly.

The preventive check appears to operate in some degree through all the ranks of society in England. There are some men, even in the highest rank, who are prevented from marrying by the idea of the expences that they must retrench, and the fancied pleasures that they must deprive themselves of, on the supposition of having a family. These considerations are certainly trivial; but a preventive foresight of this kind has objects of much greater weight for its contemplation as we go lower.

A man of liberal education, but with an income only just sufficient to enable him to associate in the rank of gentlemen, must feel absolutely certain that if he marries, and has a family, he shall be obliged, if he mixes at all in society, to rank himself with moderate farmers, and the lower class of tradesmen. The woman that a man of education would naturally make the object of his choice, would be one brought up in the same tastes and sentiments with himself, and used to the familiar intercourse of a society totally different from that to which she must be reduced by marriage. Can a man consent to place the object of his affection in a situation so discordant, probably, to her tastes and inclinations? Two or three steps of descent in society, particularly at this round of the ladder, where education ends and ignorance begins, will not be considered by the generality of people as a fancied and chimerical, but a real and essential evil. If society be held desirable, it surely must be free, equal, and reciprocal society, where benefits are conferred as well as received; and not such as the dependent finds with his patron, or the poor with the rich.

These considerations undoubtedly prevent a great number in this rank of life from following the bent of their inclinations in an early attachment. Others, guided either by a stronger passion, or a weaker judgment, break through these restraints; and it would be hard indeed if the gratification of so delightful a passion as virtuous love, did not sometimes more than counterbalance all its attendant evils. But I fear it must be owned, that the more general consequences of such marriages are rather calculated to justify, than to repress, the forebodings of the prudent.

The sons of tradesmen and farmers are exhorted not to marry, and generally find it necessary to pursue this advice, till they are settled in some business, or farm, that may enable them to support a family. These events may not, perhaps, occur till they are far advanced in life. The scarcity of farms is a very general complaint in England. And the competition in every kind of business is so great, that it is not possible that all should be successful.

The labourer who earns eighteen pence a day, and lives with some degree of comfort as a single man, will hesitate a little before he divides that pittance among four or five, which seems to be but just sufficient for one. Harder fare and harder labour he would submit to, for the sake of living with the woman that he loves; but he must feel conscious, if he thinks at all, that, should he have a large family, and any ill luck whatever, no degree of frugality, no possible exertion of his manual strength, could preserve him from the heart-rending sensation of seeing his children starve, or of forfeiting his independence, and being obliged to the parish for their support. The love of independence is a sentiment that surely none would wish to be erased from the breast of man : though the parish law of England, it must be confessed, is a system of all others the most calculated gradually to weaken this sentiment, and in the end, may eradicate it completely.

The servants who live in gentlemen's families, have restraints that are yet stronger to break through, in venturing upon marriage. They possess the necessaries, and even the comforts of life, almost in as great plenty as their masters. Their work is easy, and their food luxurious, compared with the class of labourers. And their sense of dependence is weakened by the conscious power of changing their masters, if they feel themselves offended. Thus comfortably situated at present, what are their prospects in marrying. Without knowledge or capital, either for business, or farming, and unused, and therefore unable to earn a subsistence by daily labour, their only refuge seems to be a miserable alehouse, which certainly offers no very enchanting prospect of a happy evening to their lives. By much the greater part, therefore, deterred by this uninviting view of their future situation, content themselves with remaining single where they are.

If this sketch of the state of society in England be near the truth, and I do not conceive that it is exaggerated, it will be allowed, that the preventive check to population in this country operates, though with varied force, through all the classes of the community. The same observation will hold true with regard to all old states. The effects, indeed, of these restraints upon marriage are but too conspicuous in the consequent vices that are produced in almost every part of the world ; vices that are continually involving both sexes in inextricable unhappiness.

CHAPTER V.

The second, or positive check to population examined, in England. —
The true cause why the immense sum collected in England for the
poor does not better their condition. — The powerful tendency of the
poor laws to defeat their own purpose. — Palliative of the distress of
the poor proposed. — The absolute impossibility from the fixed laws of
our nature, that the pressure of want can ever be completely re-
moved from the lower classes of society. — All the checks to population
may be resolved into misery or vice.

THE positive check to population, by which I mean, the
check which represses an increase which is already begun, is
confined chiefly, though not perhaps solely, to the lowest
orders of society. This check is not so obvious to common
view as the other I have mentioned ; and, to prove distinctly
the force and extent of its operation, would require, perhaps,
more data than we are in possession of. But I believe it
has been very generally remarked by those who have attended to bills of mortality, that of the number of children
who die annually, much too great a proportion belongs to
those, who may be supposed unable to give their offspring
proper food and attention ; exposed as they are occasionally
to severe distress, and confined, perhaps, to unwholesome
habitations and hard labour. This mortality among the
children of the poor has been constantly taken notice of in
all towns. It certainly does not prevail in an equal degree

in the country; but the subject has not hitherto received sufficient attention to enable any one to say, that there are not more deaths in proportion, among the children of the poor, even in the country, than among those of the middling and higher classes. Indeed it seems difficult to suppose that a labourer's wife, who has six children, and who is sometimes in absolute want of bread, should be able always to give them the food and attention necessary to support life. The sons and daughters of peasants will not be found such rosy cherubs in real life, as they are described to be in romances. It cannot fail to be remarked by those who live much in the country, that the sons of labourers are very apt to be stunted in their growth, and are a long while arriving at maturity. Boys that you would guess to be fourteen or fifteen, are upon inquiry, frequently found to be eighteen or nineteen. And the lads who drive ploughs, which must certainly be a healthy exercise, are very rarely seen with any appearance of calves to their legs; a circumstance which can only be attributed to a want of proper, or of sufficient nourishment.

To remedy the frequent distress of the common people, the poor laws of England have been instituted; but it is to be feared, that though they may have alleviated a little the intensity of individual misfortune, they have spread the general evil over a much larger surface. It is a subject often started in conversation, and mentioned always as a matter of great surprise, that notwithstanding the immense sum that is annually collected for the poor in England, there is still so much distress among them. Some think that the money must be embezzled; others that the churchwardens and

overseers consume the greater part of it in dinners. All
agree that some how or other it must be very ill-managed.
In short the fact, that nearly three millions are collected
annually for the poor, and yet that their distresses are not
removed, is the subject of continual astonishment. But a
man who sees a little below the surface of things would be
very much more astonished, if the fact were otherwise than
it is observed to be, or even if a collection universally of
eighteen shillings in the pound instead of four, were materially to alter it. I will state a case which I hope will elucidate my meaning.

Suppose, that by a subscription of the rich, the eighteen
pence a day which men earn now, was made up five shillings, it might be imagined, perhaps, that they would then
be able to live comfortably, and have a piece of meat every
day for their dinners. But this would be a very false conclusion. The transfer of three shillings and sixpence a day
to every labourer, would not increase the quantity of meat
in the country. There is not at present enough for all to
have a decent share. What would then be the consequence?
The competition among the buyers in the market of meat,
would rapidly raise the price from six pence or seven pence,
to two or three shillings in the pound ; and the commodity
would not be divided among many more than it is at present. When an article is scarce, and cannot be distributed
to all, he that can shew the most valid patent, that is, he that
offers most money becomes the possessor. If we can suppose the competition among the buyers of meat to continue
long enough for a greater number of cattle to be reared
annually, this could only be done at the expence of the corn,

which would be a very disadvantageous exchange; for it is well known that the country could not then support the same population; and when subsistence is scarce in proportion to the number of people, it is of little consequence whether the lowest members of the society possess eighteen pence or five shillings. They must at all events be reduced to live upon the hardest fare, and in the smallest quantity.

It will be said, perhaps, that the increased number of purchasers in every article would give a spur to productive industry, and that the whole produce of the island would be increased. This might in some degree be the case. But the spur that these fancied riches would give to population, would more than counterbalance it, and the increased produce would be to be divided among a more than proportionably increased number of people. All this time I am supposing that the same quantity of work would be done as before. But this would not really take place. The receipt of five shillings a day, instead of eighteen pence, would make every man fancy himself comparatively rich, and able to indulge himself in many hours or days of leisure. This would give a strong and immediate check to productive industry; and in a short time, not only the nation would be poorer, but the lower classes themselves would be much more distressed than when they received only eighteen pence a day.

A collection from the rich of eighteen shillings in the pound, even if distributed in the most judicious manner, would have a little the same effect as that resulting from the supposition I have just made; and no possible contributions or sacrifices of the rich, particularly in money, could for any time prevent the recurrence of distress among the lower members of society, whoever they were. Great changes might, indeed, be made. The rich might become poor, and some of the poor rich : but a part of the society must necessarily feel a difficulty of living ; and this difficulty will naturally fall on the least fortunate members.

It may at first appear strange, but I believe it is true, that I cannot by means of money raise a poor man, and enable him to live much better than he did before, without proportionably depressing others in the same class. If I retrench the quantity of food consumed in my house, and give him what I have cut off, I then benefit him, without depressing any but myself and family, who, perhaps, may be well able to bear it. If I turn up a piece of uncultivated land, and then give him the produce, I then benefit both him, and all the members of the society, because what he before consumed is thrown into the common stock, and probably some of the new produce with it. But if I only give him money, supposing the produce of the country to remain the same, I give him a title to a larger share of that produce than formerly, which share he cannot receive without diminishing the shares of others. It is evident that this effect, in individual instances, must be so small as to be totally imperceptible ; but still it must exist, as many other effects do, which like some of the insects which people the air, elude our grosser perceptions.

Supposing the quantity of food in any country to remain the same for many years together ; it is evident that this food must be divided according to the value of each man's patent,* or the sum of money that he can afford to spend in this commodity so universally in request. It is a demonstrative truth therefore, that the patents of one set of men could not be increased in value, without diminishing the value of the patents of some other set of men. If the rich were to subscribe, and give five shillings a day to five hundred thousand men without retrenching their own tables, no doubt can exist, that as these men would naturally live more at their ease, and consume a greater quantity of provisions, there would be less food remaining to divide among the rest; and consequently each man's patent would be diminished in value, or the same number of pieces of silver would purchase a smaller quantity of subsistence.

An increase of population without a proportionate increase of food, will evidently have the same effect in lowering the value of each man's patent. The food must necessarily be distributed in smaller quantities, and consequently a day's labour will purchase a smaller quantity of provisions. An increase in the price of provisions would arise, either from an increase of population faster than the means of subsistence; or from a different distribution of the money of the society. The food of a country that has been long occupied, if it be increasing, increases slowly and regularly, and cannot be made to answer any sudden demands; but variations in the distribution of the money of a society are not unfrequently occurring, and are undoubtedly among the

---

* Mr. Godwin calls the wealth that a man received from his ancestors a mouldy patent. It may, I think, very properly be termed a patent; but I hardly see the propriety of calling it a mouldy one, as it is an article in such constant use.

causes that occasion the continual variations which we ob
serve in the price of provisions.

The poor-laws of England tend to depress the genera
condition of the poor in these two ways. Their first obvi
ous tendency is to increase population without increasin
the food for its support. A poor man may marry with littl
or no prospect of being able to support a family in inde
pendence. They may be said therefore in some measur
to create the poor which they maintain; and as the pro
visions of the country must, in consequence of the increase
population, be distributed to every man in smaller propor
tions, it is evident that the labour of those who are not sup
ported by parish assistance, will purchase a smaller quantit
of provisions than before, and consequently, more of then
must be driven to ask for support.

Secondly, the quantity of provisions consumed in work
houses upon a part of the society, that cannot be consid
ered in general as the most valuable part, diminishes th
shares that would otherwise belong to more industrious, an
more worthy members; and thus in the same manner force
more to become dependent. If the poor in the workhouse
were to live better than they now do, this new distributio
of the money of the society would tend more conspicu
ously to depress the condition of those out of the work
houses, by occasioning a rise in the price of provisions.

Fortunately for England, a spirit of independence sti
remains among the peasantry. The poor-laws are strongl
calculated to eradicate this spirit. They have succeeded i
part; but had they succeeded as completely as might hav

been expected, their pernicious tendency would not have been so long concealed.

Hard as it may appear in individual instances, dependent poverty ought to be held disgraceful. Such a stimulus seems to be absolutely necessary to promote the happiness of the great mass of mankind; and every general attempt to weaken this stimulus, however benevolent its apparent intention, will always defeat its own purpose. If men are induced to marry from a prospect of parish provision, with little or no chance of maintaining their families in independence, they are not only unjustly tempted to bring unhappiness and dependence upon themselves and children; but they are tempted, without knowing it, to injure all in the same class with themselves. A labourer who marries without being able to support a family, may in some respects be considered as an enemy to all his fellow-labourers.

I feel no doubt whatever, that the parish laws of England have contributed to raise the price of provisions, and to lower the real price of labour. They have therefore contributed to impoverish that class of people whose only possession is their labour. It is also difficult to suppose that they have not powerfully contributed to generate that carelessness, and want of frugality observable among the poor, so contrary to the disposition frequently to be remarked among petty tradesmen and small farmers. The labouring poor, to use a vulgar expression, seem always to live from hand to mouth. Their present wants employ their whole attention, and they seldom think of the future. Even when they have an opportunity of saving they seldom exercise it; but all that is beyond their present necessities goes, generally speaking, to the ale-house. The poor-laws of England may therefore be said to diminish both the power and the will to save, among the common people, and thus to weaken one of the strongest incentives to sobriety and industry, and consequently to happiness.

It is a general complaint among master manufacturers, that high wages ruin all their workmen; but it is difficult to conceive that these men would not save a part of their high wages for the future support of their families, instead of spending it in drunkenness and dissipation, if they did not rely on parish assistance for support in case of accidents. And that the poor employed in manufactures consider this assistance as a reason why they may spend all the wages they earn, and enjoy themselves while they can, appears to be evident from the number of families that, upon the failure of any great manufactory, immediately fall upon the parish; when perhaps the wages earned in this manufactory, while it flourished, were sufficiently above the price of common country labour, to have allowed them to save enough for their support, till they could find some other channel for their industry.

A man who might not be deterred from going to the ale-house, from the consideration that on his death or sickness he should leave his wife and family upon the parish, might yet hesitate in thus dissipating his earnings, if he were assured that, in either of these cases, his family must starve, or be left to the support of casual bounty. In China, where the real as well as nominal price of labour is very low, sons are yet obliged by law to support their aged and helpless parents. Whether such a law would be advisable in this country, I will not pretend to determine. But it seems at any rate highly improper, by positive institutions, which render dependent poverty so general, to weaken that disgrace, which for the best and most humane reasons ought to attach to it.

The mass of happiness among the common people cannot but be diminished, when one of the strongest checks to idleness and dissipation is thus removed ; and when men are thus allured to marry with little or no prospect of being able to maintain a family in independence. Every obstacle in the way of marriage must undoubtedly be considered as a species of unhappiness. But as from the laws of our nature some check to population must exist, it is better that it should be checked from a foresight of the difficulties attending a family, and the fear of dependent poverty, than that it should be encouraged, only to be repressed afterwards by want and sickness.

It should be remembered always, that there is an essential difference between food and those wrought commodities, the raw materials of which are in great plenty. A demand for these last will not fail to create them in as great quantity as they are wanted. The demand for food has by no means the same creative power. In a country where all the fertile spots have been seized, high offers are necessary to encourage the farmer to lay his dressing on land, from which he cannot expect a profitable return for some years. And before the prospect of advantage is sufficiently great to encourage this sort of agricultural enterprise, and while the new produce is rising, great distresses may be suffered from the want of it. The demand for an increased quantity of

D

subsistence is, with few exceptions, constant everywhere, yet we see how slowly it is answered in all those countries that have been long occupied.

The poor-laws of England were undoubtedly instituted for the most benevolent purpose; but there is great reason to think that they have not succeeded in their intention. They certainly mitigate some cases of very severe distress which might otherwise occur; yet the state of the poor who are supported by parishes, considered in all its circumstances, is very far from being free from misery. But one of the principal objections to them is, that for this assistance which some of the poor receive, in itself almost a doubtful blessing, the whole class of the common people of England is subject to a set of grating, inconvenient, and tyrannical laws, totally inconsistent with the genuine spirit of the constitution. The whole business of settlements, even in its present amended state, is utterly contrary to all ideas of freedom. The parish persecution of men whose families are likely to become chargeable, and of poor women who are near lying-in, is a most disgraceful and disgusting tyranny. And the obstructions continually occasioned in the market of labour by these laws, have a constant tendency to add to the difficulties of those who are struggling to support themselves without assistance.

These evils attendant on the poor-laws are in some degree irremediable. If assistance be to be distributed to a certain class of people, a power must be given somewhere of discriminating the proper objects, and of managing the concerns of the institutions that are necessary; but any great interference with the concerns of other people, is a species of tyranny; and in the common course of things, the exercise of this power may be expected to become grating to those who are driven to ask for support. The tyranny of Justices, Churchwardens, and Overseers, is a common complaint among the poor : but the fault does not lie so much in these persons, who probably before they were in power were not worse than other people ; but in the nature of all such institutions.

The evil is perhaps gone too far to be remedied ; but I feel little doubt in my own mind, that if the poor-laws had never existed, though there might have been a few more instances of very severe distress, yet that the aggregate mass of happiness among the common people would have been much greater than it is at present.

Mr. Pitt's Poor-bill has the appearance of being framed with benevolent intentions, and the clamour raised against it was in many respects ill directed, and unreasonable. But it must be confessed that it possesses in a high degree the great and radical defect of all systems of the kind, that, of tending to increase population without increasing the means for its support, and thus to depress the condition of those that are not supported by parishes, and, consequently, to create more poor.

To remove the wants of the lower classes of society, is indeed an arduous task. The truth is, that the pressure of distress on this part of a community is an evil so deeply seated, that no human ingenuity can reach it. Were I to propose a palliative ; and palliatives are all that the nature of the case will admit ; it should be, in the first place, the total abolition of all the present parish-laws. This would at any rate give liberty and freedom of action to the peasantry of England, which they can hardly be said to possess at present. They would then be able to settle without interruption, wherever there was a prospect of a greater plenty of work, and a higher price for labour. The market of labour would then be free, and those obstacles removed, which as things are now, often for a considerable time prevent the price from rising according to the demand.

Secondly, Premiums might be given for turning up fresh land, and all possible encouragements held out to agriculture above manufactures, and to tillage above grazing. Every endeavour should be used to weaken and destroy all those institutions relating to corporations, apprenticeships, etc., which cause the labours of agriculture to be worse paid than the labours of trade and manufactures. For a country can never produce its proper quantity of food while these distinctions remain in favour of artizans. Such encouragements to agriculture would tend to furnish the market with an increasing quantity of healthy work, and at the same time, by augmenting the produce of the country, would raise the comparative price of labour, and ameliorate the condition of the labourer. Being now in better circumstances, and seeing no prospect of parish assistance, he would be more able, as well as more inclined, to enter into associations for providing against the sickness of himself or family.

Lastly, for cases of extreme distress, county workhouses might be established, supported by rates upon the whole kingdom, and free for persons of all counties, and indeed of all nations. The fare should be hard, and those that were able obliged to work. It would be desirable, that they should not be considered as comfortable asylums in all difficulties; but merely places where severe distress might find some alleviation. A part of these houses might be separated, or others built for a more beneficial purpose, which has not been unfrequently taken notice of, that of providing a place, where any person, whether native or foreign, might do a day's work at all times, and receive the market price for it. Many cases would undoubtedly be left for the exertion of individual benevolence.

A plan of this kind, the preliminary of which, should be an abolition of all the present parish-laws, seems to be the best calculated to increase the mass of happiness among the common people of England. To prevent the recurrence of misery, is, alas! beyond the power of man. In the vain endeavour to obtain what in the nature of things is impossible, we now sacrifice not only possible but certain benefits. We tell the common people, that if they will submit to a code of tyrannical regulations, they shall never be in want. They do submit to these regulations. They perform their part of the contract: but we do not, nay cannot, perform ours: and thus the poor sacrifice the valuable blessing of liberty, and receive nothing that can be called an equivalent in return.

Notwithstanding then, the institution of the poor-laws in England, I think it will be allowed, that considering the state of the lower classes altogether, both in the towns and in the country, the distresses which they suffer from the want of proper and sufficient food, from hard labour and unwholesome habitations, must operate as a constant check to incipient population.

To these two great checks to population, in all long occupied countries, which I have called the preventive and the positive checks, may be added vicious customs with respect to women, great cities, unwholesome manufactures, luxury, pestilence, and war.

All these checks may be fairly resolved into misery and vice.

And that these are the true causes of the slow increase of population in all the states of modern Europe, will appear sufficiently evident from the comparatively rapid increase that has invariably taken place, whenever these causes have been in any considerable degree removed.

CHAPTER VII.

. . Best criterion of a permanent increase of population. — Great frugality of living one of the causes of the famines of China and Indostan. — Evil tendency of one of the clauses of Mr. Pitt's Poor Bill. — Only one proper way of encouraging population. — Causes of the happiness of nations. — Famine, the last and most dreadful mode by which nature represses a redundant population. — The three propositions considered as established.

. . . The passion between the sexes has appeared in every age to be so nearly the same, that it may always be considered, in algebraic language, as a given quantity. The great law of necessity which prevents population from increasing in any country beyond the food which it can either produce or acquire, is a law, so open to our view, so obvious and evident to our understandings, and so completely confirmed by the experience of every age, that we cannot for a moment doubt it. The different modes which nature takes to prevent, or repress a redundant population, do not appear, indeed, to us so certain and regular ; but though we cannot always predict the mode, we may with certainty predict the fact. If the proportion of births to deaths for a few years, indicate an increase of numbers much beyond the proportional increased or acquired produce of the country, we may be perfectly certain, that unless an emigration takes place,

39

the deaths will shortly exceed the births; and that the increase that had taken place for a few years cannot be the real average increase of the population of the country. Were there no other depopulating causes, every country would, without doubt, be subject to periodical pestilences or famines.

The only true criterion of a real and permanent increase in the population of any country, is the increase of the means of subsistence. But even this criterion is subject to some slight variations, which are, however, completely open to our view and observations. In some countries population seems to have been forced; that is, the people have been habituated by degrees to live almost upon the smallest possible quantity of food. There must have been periods in such countries, when population increased permanently, without an increase in the means of subsistence. China seems to answer to this description. If the accounts we have of it are to be trusted, the lower classes of people are in the habit of living almost upon the smallest possible quantity of food, and are glad to get any putrid offals that European labourers would rather starve than eat. The law in China which permits parents to expose their children, has tended principally thus to force the population. A nation in this state must necessarily be subject to famines. Where a country is so populous in proportion to the means of subsistence, that the average produce of it is but barely sufficient to support the lives of the inhabitants, any deficiency from the badness of seasons must be fatal. It is probable that the very frugal manner in which the Gentoos are in the habit of living contributes in some degree to the famines of Indostan.

In America, where the reward of labour is at present so liberal, the lower classes might retrench very considerably in a year of scarcity, without materially distressing themselves. A famine therefore seems to be almost impossible. It may be expected, that in the progress of the population of America, the labourers will in time be much less liberally rewarded. The numbers will in this case permanently increase, without a proportional increase in the means of subsistence.

In the different States of Europe there must be some variations in the proportion between the number of inhabitants, and the quantity of food consumed, arising from the different habits of living that prevail in each State. The labourers of the South of England are so accustomed to eat fine wheaten bread, that they will suffer themselves to be half starved, before they will submit to live like the Scotch peasants. They might perhaps in time, by the constant operation of the hard law of necessity, be reduced to live even like the lower Chinese : and the country would then, with the same quantity of food, support a greater population. But to effect this must always be a most difficult, and every friend to humanity will hope, an abortive attempt. Nothing is so common as to hear of encouragements that ought to be given to population. If the tendency of mankind to increase be so great as I have represented it to be, it may seem strange that this increase does not come when it is thus repeatedly called for. The true reason is, that the demand for a greater population is made without preparing the funds necessary to support it. Increase the demand for agricultural labour by promoting cultivation, and with it consequently increase the produce of the country, and ameliorate the condition of the labourer, and no apprehensions whatever need be entertained of the proportional increase of population. An attempt to effect this purpose in any other way is vicious, cruel, and tyrannical, and in any state of tolerable freedom cannot therefore succeed. It may appear to be the interest of the rulers, and the rich of a State, to force population, and thereby lower the price of labour, and consequently the expence of fleets and armies, and the cost of manufactures for foreign sale: but every attempt of the kind should be carefully watched, and strenuously resisted by the friends of the poor, particularly when it comes under the deceitful garb of benevolence, and is likely, on that account, to be cheerfully and cordially received by the common people.

I entirely acquit Mr. Pitt of any sinister intention in that clause of his poor bill which allows a shilling a week to every labourer for each child he has above three. I confess, that before the bill was brought into Parliament, and for some time after, I thought that such a regulation would be highly beneficial; but further reflection on the subject has convinced me, that if its object be to better the condition of the poor, it is calculated to defeat the very purpose which it has in view. It has no tendency that I can discover to increase the produce of the country; and if it tend to increase population, without increasing the produce, the necessary and inevitable consequence appears to be, that the same produce must be divided among a greater number, and consequently that a day's labour will purchase a smaller quantity of provisions, and the poor therefore in general must be more distressed.

I have mentioned some cases, where population may permanently increase, without a proportional increase in the means of subsistence. But it is evident that the variation in different States, between the food and the numbers supported by it, is restricted to a limit beyond which it cannot pass. In every country, the population of which is not absolutely decreasing, the food must be necessarily sufficient to support, and to continue, the race of labourers.

Other circumstances being the same, it may be affirmed, that countries are populous, according to the quantity of human food which they produce; and happy, according to the liberality with which that food is divided, or the quantity which a day's labour will purchase. Corn countries are more populous than pasture countries; and rice countries more populous than corn countries. The lands in England are not suited to rice, but they would all bear potatoes: and Dr. Adam Smith observes, that if potatoes were to become the favourite vegetable food of the common people, and if the same quantity of land was employed in their culture as is now employed in the culture of corn, the country would be able to support a much greater population; and would consequently in a very short time have it.

The happiness of a country does not depend, absolutely, upon its poverty or its riches, upon its youth or its age, upon its being thinly or fully inhabited, but upon the rapidity with which it is increasing, upon the degree in which the yearly increase of food approaches to the yearly increase of an unrestricted population. This approximation is always the nearest in new colonies, where the knowledge and industry of an old State, operate on the fertile unappropriated land of the new one. In other cases, the youth or age of a State is not in this respect of very great importance. It is probable, that the food of Great Britain is divided in as great plenty to the inhabitants, at the present period, as it was two thousand, three thousand, or four thousand years ago. And there is reason to believe that the poor and thinly inhabited tracts of the Scotch Highlands, are as much distressed by an overcharged population, as the rich and populous province of Flanders.

Were a country never to be over-run by a people more advanced in arts, but left to its own natural progress in civilization ; from the time that its produce might be considered as an unit, to the time that it might be considered as a million, during the lapse of many hundred years, there would not be a single period, when the mass of the people could be said to be free from distress, either directly or indirectly, for want of food. In every State in Europe, since we have first had accounts of it, millions and millions of human existences have been repressed from this simple cause ; though perhaps in some of these States, an absolute famine has never been known.

Famine seems to be the last, the most dreadful resource of nature. The power of population is so superior to the power in the earth to produce subsistence for man, that premature death must in some shape or other visit the human race. The vices of mankind are active and able ministers of depopulation. They are the precursors in the great army of destruction ; and often finish the dreadful work themselves. But should they fail in this war of extermination, sickly seasons, epidemics, pestilence, and plague, advance in terrific array, and sweep off their thousands and ten thousands. Should success be still incomplete ; gigantic inevitable famine stalks in the rear, and with one mighty blow, levels the population with the food of the world.

Must it not then be acknowledged by an attentive examiner of the histories of mankind, that in every age and in every State in which man has existed, or does now exist,

That the increase of population is necessarily limited by the means of subsistence.

That population does invariably increase when the means of subsistence increase. And,

That the superior power of population is repressed, and the actual population kept equal to the means of subsistence by misery and vice.

CHAPTER X.

In reading Mr. Godwin's ingenious and able work on
political justice, it is impossible not to be struck with the
spirit and energy of his style, the force and precision of
some of his reasonings, the ardent tone of his thoughts, and
particularly with that impressive earnestness of manner
which gives an air of truth to the whole. At the same time,
it must be confessed, that he has not proceeded in his enquiries with the caution that sound philosophy seems to
require. His conclusions are often unwarranted by his
premises. He fails sometimes in removing the objections
which he himself brings forward. He relies too much on
general and abstract propositions which will not admit of
application. And his conjectures certainly far outstrip the
modesty of nature.

The system of equality which Mr. Godwin proposes is,
without doubt, by far the most beautiful and engaging of
any that has yet appeared. An amelioration of society to
be produced merely by reason and conviction, wears much

more the promise of permanence, than any change effected and maintained by force. The unlimited exercise of private judgment, is a doctrine inexpressibly grand and captivating, and has a vast superiority over those systems where every individual is in a manner the slave of the public. The substitution of benevolence as the master-spring, and moving principle of society, instead of self-love, is a consummation devoutly to be wished. In short, it is impossible to contemplate the whole of this fair structure, without emotions of delight and admiration, accompanied with ardent longing for the period of its accomplishment. But, alas! that moment can never arrive. The whole is little better than a dream, a beautiful phantom of the imagination. These "gorgeous palaces" of happiness and immortality, these "solemn temples" of truth and virtue will dissolve, "like the baseless fabric of a vision," when we awaken to real life, and contemplate the true and genuine situation of man on earth.

Mr. Godwin, at the conclusion of the third chapter of his eighth book, speaking of population, says, "There is a principle in human society, by which population is perpetually kept down to the level of the means of subsistence. Thus among the wandering tribes of America and Asia, we never find through the lapse of ages that population has so increased as to render necessary the cultivation of the earth." This principle, which Mr. Godwin thus mentions as some mysterious and occult cause, and which he does not attempt to investigate, will be found to be the grinding law of necessity; misery, and the fear of misery.

The great error under which Mr. Godwin labours throughout his whole work, is, the attributing almost all the vices and misery that are seen in civil society to human institutions. Political regulations, and the established administration of property, are with him the fruitful sources of all evil, the hotbeds of all the crimes that degrade mankind. Were this really a true state of the case, it would not seem a hopeless task to remove evil completely from the world; and reason seems to be the proper and adequate instrument for effecting so great a purpose. But the truth is, that though human institutions appear to be the obvious and obtrusive causes of much mischief to mankind; yet, in reality, they are light and superficial, they are mere feathers that float on the surface, in comparison with those deeper seated causes of impurity that corrupt the springs, and render turbid the whole stream of human life.

Mr. Godwin, in his chapter on the benefits attendant on a system of equality, says, "The spirit of oppression, the spirit of servility, and the spirit of fraud, these are the immediate growth of the established administration of property. They are alike hostile to intellectual improvement. The other vices of envy, malice, and revenge, are their inseparable companions. In a state of society, where men lived in the midst of plenty, and where all shared alike the bounties of nature, these sentiments would inevitably expire. The narrow principle of selfishness would vanish. No man being obliged to guard his little store, or provide with anxiety and pain for his restless wants, each would lose his individual existence in the thought of the general good. No man would be an enemy to his neighbour, for they would have no subject of contention; and, of consequence, philanthropy would resume the empire which reason assigns her. Mind would be delivered from her perpetual anxiety about corporal support, and free to expatiate in the field of thought, which is congenial to her. Each would assist the enquiries of all."

This would, indeed, be a happy state. But that it is merely an imaginary picture, with scarcely a feature near the truth, the reader, I am afraid, is already too well convinced.

Man cannot live in the midst of plenty. All cannot share alike the bounties of nature. Were there no established administration of property, every man would be obliged to guard with force his little store. Selfishness would be triumphant. The subjects of contention would be perpetual. Every individual mind would be under a constant anxiety about corporal support; and not a single intellect would be left free to expatiate in the field of thought.

How little Mr. Godwin has turned the attention of his penetrating mind to the real state of man on earth, will sufficiently appear from the manner in which he endeavours to remove the difficulty of an overcharged population. He says, "The obvious answer to this objection, is, that to reason thus is to foresee difficulties at a great distance. Three-fourths of the habitable globe is now uncultivated. The parts already cultivated are capable of immeasurable improvement. Myriads of centuries of still increasing population may pass away, and the earth be still found sufficient for the subsistence of its inhabitants."

I have already pointed out the error of supposing that no distress and difficulty would arise from an overcharged population before the earth absolutely refused to produce any

E

more.　But let us imagine for a moment Mr. Godwin's beautiful system of equality realized in its utmost purity, and see how soon this difficulty might be expected to press under so perfect a form of society.　A theory that will not admit of application cannot possibly be just.

Let us suppose all the causes of misery and vice in this island removed.　War and contention cease.　Unwholesome trades and manufactories do not exist.　Crowds no longer collect together in great and pestilent cities for purposes of court intrigue, of commerce, and vicious gratifications. Simple, healthy, and rational amusements take place of drinking, gaming and debauchery.　There are no towns sufficiently large to have any prejudicial effects on the human constitution.　The greater part of the happy inhabitants of this terrestrial paradise live in hamlets and farm-houses scattered over the face of the country.　Every house is clean, airy, sufficiently roomy, and in a healthy situation.　All men are equal.　The labours of luxury are at end.　And the necessary labours of agriculture are shared amicably among all.　The number of persons, and the produce of the island, we suppose to be the same as at present. The spirit of benevolence, guided by impartial justice, will divide this produce among all the members of the society according to their wants.　Though it would be impossible that they should all have animal food every day, yet vegetable food, with meat occasionally, would satisfy the desires of a frugal people, and would be sufficient to preserve them in health, strength, and spirits.

Mr. Godwin considers marriage as a fraud and a monopoly.　Let us suppose the commerce of the sexes established upon principles of the most perfect freedom. Mr. Godwin does not think himself that this freedom would lead to a promiscuous intercourse ; and in this I perfectly agree with him. The love of variety is a vicious, corrupt, and unnatural taste, and could not prevail in any great degree in a simple and virtuous state of society. Each man would probably select himself a partner, to whom he would adhere as long as that adherence continued to be the choice of both parties. It would be of little consequence, according to Mr. Godwin, how many children a woman had, or to whom they belonged. Provisions and assistance would spontaneously flow from the quarter in which they abounded to the quarter that was deficient.* And every man would be ready to furnish instruction to the rising generation according to his capacity.

I cannot conceive a form of society so favourable upon the whole to population. The irremediableness of marriage, as it is at present constituted, undoubtedly deters many from entering into that state. An unshackled intercourse, on the contrary, would be a most powerful incitement to early attachments : and as we are supposing no anxiety about the future support of children to exist, I do not conceive that there would be one woman in a hundred, of twenty-three, without a family.

With these extraordinary encouragements to population, and every cause of depopulation, as we have supposed, removed, the numbers would necessarily increase faster than in any society that has ever yet been known. I have mentioned, on the authority of a pamphlet published by a Dr.

* See B. 8.   Chap. 8.   P. 504.

Styles, and referred to by Dr. Price, that the inhabitants of the back settlements of America doubled their numbers in fifteen years. England is certainly a more healthy country than the back settlements of America; and as we have supposed every house in the island to be airy and wholesome, and the encouragements to have a family greater even than with the back settlers, no probable reason can be assigned, why the population should not double itself in less, if possible, than fifteen years. But to be quite sure that we do not go beyond the truth, we will only suppose the period of doubling to be twenty-five years, a ratio of increase, which is well known to have taken place throughout all the Northern States of America.

There can be little doubt, that the equalization of property which we have supposed, added to the circumstance of the labour of the whole community being directed chiefly to agriculture, would tend greatly to augment the produce of the country. But to answer the demands of a population increasing so rapidly, Mr. Godwin's calculation of half an hour a day for each man, would certainly not be sufficient. It is probable that the half of every man's time must be employed for this purpose. Yet with such, or much greater exertions, a person who is acquainted with the nature of the soil in this country, and who reflects on the fertility of the lands already in cultivation, and the barrenness of those that are not cultivated, will be very much disposed to doubt, whether the whole average produce could possibly be doubled in twenty-five years from the present period. The only chance of success would be the ploughing up all the grazing countries, and putting an end almost entirely to the use of animal food. Yet a part of this scheme might defeat itself. The soil of England will not produce much without dressing; and cattle seem to be necessary to make that species of manure which best suits the land. In China, it is said that the soil in some of the provinces is so fertile, as to produce two crops of rice in the year without dressing. None of the lands in England will answer to this description.

Difficult, however, as it might be, to double the average produce of the island in twenty-five years, let us suppose it effected. At the expiration of the first period, therefore, the food, though almost entirely vegetable, would be sufficient to support in health, the doubled population of fourteen millions.

During the next period of doubling, where will the food be found to satisfy the importunate demands of the increasing numbers? Where is the fresh land to turn up? where is the dressing necessary to improve that which is already in cultivation? There is no person with the smallest knowledge of land, but would say, that it is impossible that the average produce of the country could be increased during the second twenty-five years by a quantity equal to what it at present yields. Yet we will suppose this increase, however improbable, to take place. The exuberant strength of the argument allows of almost any concession. Even with this concession, however, there would be seven millions at the expiration of the second term, unprovided for. A quantity of food equal to the frugal support of twenty-one millions, would be to be divided among twenty-eight millions.

Alas! what becomes of the picture where men lived in the midst of plenty : where no man was obliged to provide with anxiety and pain for his restless wants : where the narrow principle of selfishness did not exist : where Mind was delivered from her perpetual anxiety about corporal support, and free to expatiate in the field of thought which is congenial to her.   This beautiful fabric of imagination vanishes at the severe touch of truth.   The spirit of benevolence, cherished and invigorated by plenty, is repressed by the chilling breath of want.   The hateful passions that had vanished reappear.   The mighty law of self-preservation expels all the softer and more exalted emotions of the soul. The temptations to evil are too strong for human nature to resist.   The corn is plucked before it is ripe, or secreted in unfair proportions ; and the whole black train of vices that belong to falsehood are immediately generated.   Provisions no longer flow in for the support of the mother with a large family.   The children are sickly from insufficient food.   The rosy flush of health gives place to the pallid cheek and hollow eye of misery.   Benevolence yet lingers in a few bosoms, makes some faint expiring struggles, till at length self-love resumes his wonted empire, and lords it triumphant over the world.

No human institutions here existed, to the perverseness of which Mr. Godwin ascribes the original sin of the worst men.*   No opposition had been produced by them between public and private good.   No monopoly has been created of those advantages which reason directs to be left in common. No man had been goaded to the breach of order by unjust laws.   Benevolence had established her reign in all hearts : and yet in so short a period as within fifty years, violence,

* B. 8.   Chap. 3.   P. 340.

oppression, falsehood, misery, every hateful vice and every form of distress, which degrade the present state of society, seem to have been generated by the most imperious circumstances, by laws inherent in the nature of man, and absolutely independent of all human regulations.

If we are not yet too well convinced of the reality of this melancholy picture, let us but look for a moment into the next period of twenty-five years; and we shall see twenty-eight millions of human beings without the means of support; and before the conclusion of the first century, the population would be one hundred and twelve millions, and the food only sufficient for thirty-five millions, leaving seventy-seven millions unprovided for. In these ages want would be indeed triumphant, and rapine and murder must reign at large: and yet all this time we are supposing the produce of the earth absolutely unlimited, and the yearly increase greater than the boldest speculator can imagine.

This is undoubtedly a very different view of the difficulty arising from population, from that which Mr. Godwin gives, when he says, " Myriads of centuries of still increasing population may pass away, and the earth be still found sufficient for the subsistence of its inhabitants."

I am sufficiently aware that the redundant twenty-eight millions, or seventy-seven millions, that I have mentioned, could never have existed. It is a perfectly just observation of Mr. Godwin, that, "There is a principle in human society, by which population is perpetually kept down to the level of the means of subsistence." The sole question is, what is this principle? Is it some obscure and occult cause? Is it some mysterious interference of heaven, which at a certain period strikes the men with impotence, and the women with barrenness? Or is it a cause, open to our researches, within our view, a cause, which has constantly been observed to operate, though with varied force, in every state in which man has been placed? Is it not a degree of misery, the necessary and inevitable result of the laws of nature, which human institutions, so far from aggravating, have tended considerably to mitigate, though they never can remove.

It may be curious to observe, in the case that we have been supposing, how some of the laws which at present govern civilized society, would be successively dictated by the most imperious necessity. As man, according to Mr. Godwin, is the creature of the impressions to which he is subject, the goadings of want could not continue long, before some violations of public or private stock would necessarily take place. As these violations increased in number and extent, the more active and comprehensive intellects of the society would soon perceive, that while population was fast increasing, the yearly produce of the country would shortly begin to diminish. The urgency of the case would suggest the necessity of some immediate measures to be taken for the general safety. Some kind of convention would then be called, and the dangerous situation of the country stated in the strongest terms. It would be observed, that while they lived in the midst of plenty, it was of little consequence who laboured the least, or who possessed the least, as every man was perfectly willing and ready to supply the wants of his neighbour. But that the question was no longer, whether one man should give to another that which he did not use himself; but whether he should give to his neighbour the

od which was absolutely necessary to his own existence.
t would be represented, that the number of those that were
n want very greatly exceeded the number and means of
hose who should supply them : that these pressing wants,
which from the state of the produce of the country could not
ll be gratified, had occasioned some flagrant violations of
istice : that these violations had already checked the in-
rease of food, and would, if they were not by some means
r other prevented, throw the whole community in confu-
ion : that imperious necessity seemed to dictate that a
early increase of produce should, if possible, be obtained
t all events : that in order to effect this first, great, and in-
dispensable purpose, it would be advisable to make a more
omplete division of land, and to secure every man's stock
gainst violation, by the most powerful sanctions, even by
death itself.

It might be urged perhaps by some objectors, that, as the
ertility of the land increased, and various accidents occurred,
he share of some men might be much more than sufficient
or their support, and that when the reign of self-love was
once established, they would not distribute their surplus
produce without some compensation in return. It would
be observed, in answer, that this was an inconvenience
greatly to be lamented ; but that it was an evil which bore
no comparison to the black train of distresses that would
nevitably be occasioned by the insecurity of property : that
the quantity of food which one man could consume, was
necessarily limited by the narrow capacity of the human
stomach : that it was not certainly probable that he should
throw away the rest ; but that even if he exchanged his sur-

plus food for the labour of others, and made them in some degree dependent on him, this would still be better than that these others should absolutely starve.

It seems highly probable, therefore, that an administration of property, not very different from that which prevails in civilized States at present, would be established, as the best, though inadequate, remedy, for the evils which were pressing on the society.

The next subject that would come under discussion, intimately connected with the preceding, is, the commerce between the sexes. It would be urged by those who had turned their attention to the true cause of the difficulties under which the community laboured, that while every man felt secure that all his children would be well provided for by general benevolence, the powers of the earth would be absolutely inadequate to produce food for the population which would inevitably ensue : that even, if the whole attention and labour of the society were directed to this sole point, and if, by the most perfect security of property, and every other encouragement that could be thought of, the greatest possible increase of produce were yearly obtained ; yet still, that the increase of food would by no means keep pace with the much more rapid increase of population : that some check to population therefore was imperiously called for : that the most natural and obvious check seemed to be, to make every man provide for his own children : that this would operate in some respect, as a measure and guide, in the increase of population ; as it might be expected that no man would bring beings into the world, for whom he could not find the means of support : that where this, notwith-

standing, was the case, it seemed necessary, for the example
of others, that the disgrace and inconvenience attending
such a conduct, should fall upon that individual who had
thus inconsiderately plunged himself and innocent children
in misery and want.

The institution of marriage, or at least, of some express
or implied obligation on every man to support his own children, seems to be the natural result of these reasonings in
a community under the difficulties that we have supposed.

The view of these difficulties presents us with a very
natural origin of the superior disgrace which attends a
breach of chastity in the woman, than in the man. It could
not be expected that women should have resources sufficient
to support their own children. When, therefore, a woman
was connected with a man, who had entered into no compact to maintain her children, and aware of the inconven-
iences that he might bring upon himself, had deserted her,
these children must necessarily fall for support upon the
society, or starve. And to prevent the frequent recurrence
of such an inconvenience, as it would be highly unjust to
punish so natural a fault by personal restraint or infliction,
the men might agree to punish it with disgrace. The
offence is besides more obvious and conspicuous in the
woman, and less liable to any mistake. The father of a
child may not always be known, but the same uncertainty
cannot easily exist with regard to the mother. Where the
evidence of the offence was most complete, and the inconvenience to the society at the same time the greatest, there,
it was agreed, that the largest share of blame should fall.
The obligation of every man to maintain his children, the

society would enforce, if there were occasion; and the greater degree of inconvenience or labour, to which a family would necessarily subject him, added to some portion of disgrace which every human being must incur, who leads another into unhappiness, might be considered as a sufficient punishment for the man.

That a woman should at present be almost driven from society, for an offence, which men commit nearly with impunity, seems to be undoubtedly a breach of natural justice. But the origin of the custom, as the most obvious and effectual method of preventing the frequent recurrence of a serious inconvenience to a community, appears to be natural, though not perhaps perfectly justifiable. This origin, however, is now lost in the new train of ideas which the custom has since generated. What at first might be dictated by state necessity, is now supported by female delicacy; and operates with the greatest force on that part of society, where, if the original intention of the custom were preserved, there is the least real occasion for it.

When these two fundamental laws of society, the security of property and the institution of marriage, were once established, inequality of conditions must necessarily follow. Those who were born after the division of property, would come into a world already possessed. If their parents, from having too large a family, could not give them sufficient for their support, what are they to do in a world where everything is appropriated? We have seen the fatal effects that would result to a society, if every man had a valid claim to an equal share of the produce of the earth. The members of a family which was grown too large for the original division of land appropriated to it, could not then demand a part of the surplus produce of others, as a debt of justice. It has appeared, that from the inevitable laws of our nature, some human beings must suffer from want. These are the unhappy persons who, in the great lottery of life, have drawn a blank. The numbers of these claimants would soon exceed the ability of the surplus produce to supply. Moral merit is a very difficult distinguishing criterion, except in extreme cases. The owners of surplus produce would in general seek some more obvious mark of distinction. And it seems both natural and just, that except upon particular occasions, their choice should fall upon those who were able, and professed themselves willing, to exert their strength in procuring a further surplus produce ; and thus at once benefiting the community, and enabling these proprietors to afford assistance to greater numbers. All who were in want of food would be urged by imperious necessity to offer their labour in exchange for this article so absolutely essential to existence. The fund appropriated to the maintenance of labour, would be, the aggregate quantity of food possessed by the owners of land beyond their own consumption. When the demands upon this fund were great and numerous, it would naturally be divided in very small shares. Labour would be ill paid. Men would offer to work for a bare subsistence, and the rearing of families would be checked by sickness and misery. On the contrary, when this fund was increasing fast ; when it was great in proportion to the numbers of claimants ; it would be divided in much larger shares. No man would exchange his labour without receiving an ample quantity of food in return. Labourers would live in ease and comfort ; and would consequently be able to rear a numerous and vigorous offspring.

On the state of this fund, the happiness, or the degree of misery, prevailing among the lower classes of people in every known State, at present chiefly depends. And on this happiness, or degree of misery, depends the increase, stationariness, or decrease of population.

And thus it appears, that a society constituted according to the most beautiful form that imagination can conceive, with benevolence for its moving principle, instead of self-love, and with every evil disposition in all its members corrected by reason and not force, would, from the inevitable laws of nature, and not from any original depravity of man, in a very short period, degenerate into a society, constructed upon a plan not essentially different from that which prevails in every known State at present ; I mean, a society divided into a class of proprietors, and a class of labourers, and with self-love for the mainspring of the great machine.

In the supposition I have made, I have undoubtedly taken the increase of population smaller, and the increase of produce greater, than they really would be. No reason can be assigned, why, under the circumstances I have supposed, population should not increase faster than in any known instance. If then we were to take the period of doubling at fifteen years, instead of twenty-five years ; and reflect upon the labour necessary to double the produce in so short a time, even if we allow it possible ; we may venture to pronounce with certainty, that if Mr. Godwin's system of society was established in its utmost perfection, instead of myriads of centuries, not thirty years could elapse, before its utter destruction from the simple principle of population.

I have taken no notice of emigration for obvious reasons. If such societies were established in other parts of Europe, these countries would be under the same difficulties with regard to population, and could admit no fresh members into their bosoms. If this beautiful society were confined to this island, it must have degenerated strangely from its original purity, and administer but a very small portion of the happiness it proposed ; in short, its essential principle must be completely destroyed, before any of its members would voluntarily consent to leave it, and live under such governments as at present exist in Europe, or submit to the extreme hardships of first settlers in new regions. We well know, from repeated experience, how much misery and hardship men will undergo in their own country, before they can determine to desert it ; and how often the most tempting proposals of embarking for new settlements have been rejected by people who appeared to be almost starving.

AN ESSAY

ON THE

PRINCIPLE OF POPULATION;

OR,

A VIEW OF ITS PAST AND PRESENT EFFECTS

ON

HUMAN HAPPINESS;

WITH AN ENQUIRY INTO OUR PROSPECTS RESPECTING THE FUTURE
REMOVAL OR MITIGATION OF THE EVILS WHICH IT OCCASIONS.

A NEW EDITION, VERY MUCH ENLARGED

By T. R. MALTHUS, A.M.
FELLOW OF JESUS COLLEGE, CAMBRIDGE.

LONDON:

PRINTED FOR J. JOHNSON, IN ST PAUL'S CHURCHYARD,
BY T. BENSLEY, BOLT COURT, FLEET STREET.

1803.

PREFACE.

———◦◦◦———

THE Essay on the Principle of Population, which I published in 1798, was suggested, as is expressed in the preface, by a paper in Mr. Godwin's Inquirer. It was written on the spur of the occasion, and from the few materials which were then within my reach in a country situation. The only authors from whose writings I had deduced the principle, which formed the main argument of the essay, were Hume, Wallace, Dr. Adam Smith, and Dr. Price; and my object was to apply it to try the truth of those speculations on the perfectibility of man and society, which at that time excited a considerable portion of the publick attention.

In the course of the discussion, I was naturally led into some examination of the effects of this principle on the existing state of society. It appeared to account for much of that poverty and misery observable among the lower classes of people in every nation, and for those reiterated failures in the efforts of the higher classes to relieve them. The more I considered the subject in this point of view, the more importance it seemed to acquire; and this consideration, joined to the degree of publick attention which the essay excited, determined me to turn my leisure reading towards an historical examination of the effects of the principle of population on the past and present state of society; that, by illustrating the subject more generally, and drawing those inferences from it, in application to the actual state of things which experience seemed to warrant, I might give it a more practical and permanent interest.

In the course of this inquiry, I found that much more had been done than I had been aware of when I first published the essay. The poverty and misery arising from a too rapid increase of population had been distinctly seen, and the most violent remedies proposed, so long ago as the times of Plato and Aristotle. And of late years the subject has been treated in such a manner, by some of the French Economists, occasionally by Montesquieu, and, among our own writers, by Dr. Franklin, Sir James Steuart, Mr. Arthur Young, and Mr. Townsend, as to create a natural surprise, that it had not excited more of the publick attention.

Much, however, remained yet to be done. Independently of the comparison between the increase of population and food, which had not perhaps been stated with sufficient force and precision; some of the most curious and interesting parts of the subject had been either wholly omitted or treated very slightly. Though it had been stated distinctly, that population must always be kept down to the level of the means of subsistence; yet few inquiries had been made into the various modes by which this level is effected; and the principle had never been sufficiently pursued to its consequences, and those practical inferences drawn from it, which a strict examination of its effects on society appears to suggest.

These therefore are the points which I have treated most in detail in the following essay. In its present shape, it may be considered as a new work, and I should probably have published it as such, omitting the few parts of the former which I have retained, but that I wished it to form a whole of itself, and not to need a continual reference to the other. On this account I trust that no apology is necessary to the purchasers of the first edition. I should hope that there are some parts of it, not reprinted in this, which may still have their use; as they were rejected, not because I thought them all of less value than what has been inserted, but because they did not suit the different plan of treating the subject which I had adopted.

To those who either understood the subject before, or saw it distinctly on the perusal of the first edition, I am fearful that I shall appear to have treated some parts of it too much in detail, and to have been guilty of unnecessary repetitions. These faults have arisen partly from want of skill, and partly from intention. In drawing similar inferences from the state of society in a number of different countries, I found it very difficult to avoid some repetitions; and in those parts of the inquiry which led to conclusions different from our usual habits of thinking, it appeared to me that, with the slightest hope of producing conviction, it was necessary to present them to the reader's mind at different times and on different occasions. I was willing to sacrifice all pretensions to merit of composition, to the chance of making an impression on a larger class of readers.

The main principle advanced is so incontrovertible, that, if I had confined myself merely to general views, I could have entrenched myself in an impregnable fortress, and the work in this form would probably have had a much more masterly air. But such general views, though they may advance the cause of abstract truth, rarely tend to promote any practical good; and I thought that I should not do justice to the subject, and bring it fairly under discussion, if I refused to consider any of the consequences which appeared necessarily to flow from it, whatever these consequences might be. By pursuing this plan, however, I am aware that I have opened a door to many objections, and probably to much severity of criticism : but I console myself with the reflection, that even the errors into which I may have fallen, by affording a handle to argument and an additional excitement to examination, may be subservient to the important end, of bringing a subject so nearly connected with the happiness of society into more general notice.

Throughout the whole of the present work, I have so far differed in principle from the former, as to suppose another check to population possible, which does not strictly come under the head either of vice or misery; and, in the latter part, I have endeavoured to soften some of the harshest conclusions of the first essay. In doing this, I hope that I have not violated the principles of just reasoning; nor expressed any opinion respecting the probable improvement of society, in which I am not borne out by the experience of the past. To those who shall still think that any check to population whatever, would be worse than the evils which it would relieve, the conclusions of the former essay will remain in full force; and if we adopt this opinion, we shall be compelled to acknowledge that the poverty and misery which prevail among the lower classes of society are absolutely irremediable.

I have taken as much pains as I could to avoid any errors in the facts and calculations which have been produced in the course of the work. Should any of them nevertheless turn out to be false, the reader will see that they will not materially affect the general tenour of the reasoning.

From the crowd of materials which presented themselves in illustration of the first branch of the subject, I dare not flatter myself that I have selected the best, or arranged them in the most perspicuous method. To those who take an interest in moral and political questions, I hope that the novelty and importance of the subject will compensate the imperfections of its execution.

LONDON, *June* 8, 1803.

CONTENTS.

———•◇•———

BOOK I.

OF THE CHECKS TO POPULATION IN THE LESS CIVILIZED PARTS OF
THE WORLD, AND IN PAST TIMES.

BOOK II.

OF THE CHECKS TO POPULATION IN THE DIFFERENT STATES OF
MODERN EUROPE.

BOOK III.

OF THE DIFFERENT SYSTEMS OR EXPEDIENTS WHICH HAVE BEEN PRO-
POSED OR HAVE PREVAILED IN SOCIETY, AS THEY AFFECT THE
EVILS ARISING FROM THE PRINCIPLE OF POPULATION.

BOOK IV.

OF OUR FUTURE PROSPECTS RESPECTING THE REMOVAL OR MITIGATION
OF THE EVILS ARISING FROM THE PRINCIPLE OF POPULATION.

ESSAY, &c.

BOOK I.

F THE CHECKS TO POPULATION IN THE LESS CIVI-
LIZED PARTS OF THE WORLD AND IN PAST TIMES.

CHAPTER I.

*tatement of the Subject. Ratios of the Increase of Population and
Food.*

IN an inquiry concerning the improvement of society, the
10de of conducting the subject which naturally presents
self, is

1. An investigation of the causes that have hitherto im-
eded the progress of mankind towards happiness ; and,

2. An examination into the probability of the total or
artial removal of these causes in future.

To enter fully into this question, and to enumerate all the
auses that have hitherto influenced human improvement,
ould be much beyond the power of an individual. The

principal object of the present essay is to examine th
effects of one great cause intimately united with the ve
nature of man, which, though it has been constantly ar
powerfully operating since the commencement of societ
has been little noticed by the writers who have treated th
subject. The facts which establish the existence of th
cause have, indeed, been repeatedly stated and ackno
ledged ; but its natural and necessary effects have bee
almost totally overlooked ; though probably among thes
effects may be reckoned a very considerable portion
that vice and misery, and of that unequal distribution
the bounties of nature, which it has been the unceasir
object of the enlightened philanthropist in all ages
correct.

The cause to which I allude, is the constant tendency i
all animated life to increase beyond the nourishment pr
pared for it.

It is observed by Dr. Franklin, that there is no bound t
the prolific nature of plants or animals, but what is made h
their crowding and interfering with each other's means
subsistence. Were the face of the earth, he says, vacant c
other plants, it might be gradually sowed and oversprea
with one kind only ; as, for instance, with fennel : and wer
it empty of other inhabitants, it might in a few ages be re
plenished from one nation only ; as, for instance, with Eng
lishmen.[a]

This is incontrovertibly true. Throughout the anim.
and vegetable kingdoms Nature has scattered the seeds c
life abroad with the most profuse and liberal hand ; but ha

[a] Franklin's Miscell. p. 9.

been comparatively sparing in the room and the nourishment necessary to rear them. The germs of existence contained in this spot of earth, with ample food, and ample room to expand in, would fill millions of worlds in the course of a few thousand years. Necessity, that imperious, all-pervading law of nature, restrains them within the prescribed bounds. The race of plants and the race of animals shrink under this great restrictive law; and man cannot by any efforts of reason escape from it.

In plants and animals, the view of the subject is simple. They are all impelled by a powerful instinct to the increase of their species; and this instinct is interrupted by no doubts about providing for their offspring. Wherever, therefore, there is liberty, the power of increase is exerted; and the superabundant effects are repressed afterwards by want of room and nourishment, which is common to plants and animals; and among animals, by their becoming the prey of each other.

The effects of this check on man are more complicated. Impelled to the increase of his species by an equally powerful instinct, reason interrupts his career, and asks him whether he may not bring beings into the world, for whom he cannot provide the means of support. If he attend to this natural suggestion, the restriction too frequently produces vice. If he hear it not, the human race will be constantly endeavouring to increase beyond the means of subsistence. But as by that law of our nature which makes food necessary to the life of man, population can never actually increase beyond the lowest nourishment capable of supporting it; a strong check on population, from

the difficulty of acquiring food, must be constantly in operation.   This difficulty must fall somewhere ; and must neces
sarily be severely felt in some or other of the various form
of misery, or the fear of misery, by a large portion of man
kind.

That population has this constant tendency to increas
beyond the means of subsistence, and that it is kept to it
necessary level by these causes, will sufficiently appear from
a review of the different states of society in which man ha
existed.   But before we proceed to this review, the subjec
will perhaps be seen in a clearer light, if we endeavour t
ascertain what would be the natural increase of populatio
if left to exert itself with perfect freedom ; and what migh
be expected to be the rate of increase in the production
of the earth, under the most favourable circumstances o
human industry.   A comparison of these two rates of in
crease will enable us to judge of the force of that tendenc
in population to increase beyond the means of subsistence
which has been stated to exist.

It will be allowed, that no country has hitherto bee
known, where the manners were so pure and simple, and th
means of subsistence so abundant, that no check whateve
has existed to early marriages from the difficulty of provid
ing for a family ; and no waste of the human species has bee
occasioned afterwards by vicious customs, by towns, by un
healthy occupations, or too severe labour.   Consequently i
no state that we have yet known, has the power of populatio
been left to exert itself with perfect freedom.

Whether the law of marriage be instituted or not, the dic
tate of nature and virtue seems to be an early attachment t

ne woman ; and where there were no impediments of any
ind in the way of a union to which such an attachment
vould lead, and no causes of depopulation afterwards, the
ncrease of the human species would be evidently much
reater than any increase which has been hitherto known.

In the northern states of America, where the means of
ubsistence have been more ample, the manners of the people
nore pure, and the checks to early marriages fewer, than in
ny of the modern states of Europe, the population was
ound to double itself, for some successive periods every
wenty-five years. Yet, even during these periods, in some
f the towns, the deaths exceeded the births ;[a] and they
onsequently required a continued supply from the country
o support their population.

In the back settlements, where the sole employment is
griculture, and vicious customs and unwholesome occupations are little known, the population was found to
double itself in fifteen years.[b] Even this extraordinary rate
f increase is probably short of the utmost power of popu-
ation. Very severe labour is requisite to clear a fresh
country ; such situations are not in general considered as
particularly healthy ; and the inhabitants probably were occasionally subject to the incursions of the Indians, which
night destroy some lives, or at any rate diminish the fruits
of industry.

According to a table of Euler, calculated on a mortality
of 1 in 36, if the births be to the deaths in the proportion of
3 to 1, the period of doubling will be only $12\frac{4}{5}$ years. And

[a] Price's Observ. on Revers. Pay. vol. i. p. 274.
[b] Id. p. 282.

G

these proportions are not only possible suppositions, but have actually occurred for short periods in more countries than one

Sir William Petty supposes a doubling possible in so short a time as ten years.[a]

But to be perfectly sure that we are far within the truth we will take the slowest of these rates of increase, a rate in which all concurring testimonies agree, and which has been repeatedly ascertained to be from procreation only.

It may safely be pronounced therefore, that population, when unchecked, goes on doubling itself every twenty-five years, or increases in a geometrical ratio.

The rate according to which the productions of the earth may be supposed to increase, it will not be so easy to determine. Of this, however, we may be perfectly certain, that the ratio of their increase must be totally of a different nature from the ratio of the increase of population. A thousand millions are just as easily doubled every twenty-five years by the power of population as a thousand. But the food to support the increase from the greater number will by no means be obtained with the same facility. Man is necessarily confined in room. When acre has been added to acre till all the fertile land is occupied, the yearly increase of food must depend upon the melioration of the land already in possession. This is a stream, which from the nature of all soils, instead of increasing, must be gradually diminishing. But population, could it be supplied with food, would go on with unexhausted vigour; and the increase of one period would furnish the power of a greater increase the next, and this, without any limit.

[a] Polit. Arith. p. 14.

From the accounts we have of China and Japan, it may be fairly doubted, whether the best directed efforts of human industry could double the produce of these countries even once in any number of years. There are many parts of the globe, indeed, hitherto uncultivated and almost unoccupied ; but the right of exterminating, or driving into a corner where they must starve, even the inhabitants of these thinly-peopled regions, will be questioned in a moral view. The process of improving their minds and directing their industry, would necessarily be slow ; and during this time, as population would regularly keep pace with the increasing produce, it would rarely happen that a great degree of knowledge and industry would have to operate at once upon rich unappropriated soil. Even where this might take place, as it does sometimes in new colonies, a geometrical ratio increases with such extraordinary rapidity, that the advantage could not last long. If America continue increasing, which she certainly will do, though not with the same rapidity as formerly, the Indians will be driven further and further back into the country, till the whole race is ultimately exterminated.

These observations are, in a degree, applicable to all the parts of the earth where the soil is imperfectly cultivated. To exterminate the inhabitants of the greatest part of Asia and Africa, is a thought that could not be admitted for a moment. To civilize and direct the industry of the various tribes of Tartars, and Negroes, would certainly be a work of considerable time, and of variable and uncertain success.

Europe is by no means so fully peopled as it might be.

In Europe there is the fairest chance that human industry may receive its best direction. The science of agriculture has been much studied in England and Scotland ; and there is still a great portion of uncultivated land in these countries. Let us consider at what rate the produce of this island might be supposed to increase under circumstances the most favourable to improvement.

If it be allowed that by the best possible policy, and great encouragements to agriculture, the average produce of the island could be doubled in the first twenty-five years, it will be allowing, probably, a greater increase than could with reason be expected.

In the next twenty-five years, it is impossible to suppose that the produce could be quadrupled. It would be contrary to all our knowledge of the properties of land. The improvement of the barren parts would be a work of time and labour ; and it must be evident to those who have the slightest acquaintance with agricultural subjects, that in proportion as cultivation extended, the additions that could yearly be made to the former average produce, must be gradually and regularly diminishing. That we may be the better able to compare the increase of population and food, let us make a supposition, which, without pretending to accuracy, is clearly more favourable to the power of production in the earth, than any experience we have had of its qualities will warrant.

Let us suppose that the yearly additions which might be made to the former average produce, instead of decreasing, which they certainly would do, were to remain the same ; and that the produce of this island might be increased every twenty-five years, by a quantity equal to what it at present produces : the most enthusiastic speculator cannot suppose a greater increase than this. In a few centuries it would make every acre of land in the island like a garden.

If this supposition be applied to the whole earth, and if it be allowed that the subsistence for man which the earth affords might be increased every twenty-five years by a quantity equal to what it at present produces, this will be supposing a rate of increase much greater than we can imagine that any possible exertions of mankind could make it.

It may be fairly pronounced therefore, that, considering the present average state of the earth, the means of subsistence, under circumstances the most favourable to human industry, could not possibly be made to increase faster than in an arithmetical ratio.

The necessary effects of these two different rates of increase, when brought together, will be very striking. Let us call the population of this island eleven millions ; and suppose the present produce equal to the easy support of such a number. In the first twenty-five years the population would be twenty-two millions, and the food being also doubled, the means of subsistence would be equal to this increase. In the next twenty-five years, the population would be forty-four millions, and the means of subsistence only equal to the support of thirty-three millions. In the next period the population would be eighty-eight millions, and the means of subsistence just equal to the support of half that number. And, at the conclusion of the first century, the population would be a hundred and seventy-six millions, and the means of subsistence only equal to the support of fifty-five millions, leaving a population of a hundred and twenty-one millions totally unprovided for.

Taking the whole earth, instead of this island, emigration would of course be excluded; and, supposing the present population equal to a thousand millions, the human species would increase as the numbers, 1, 2, 4, 8, 16, 32, 64, 128, 256, and subsistence as 1, 2, 3, 4, 5, 6, 7, 8, 9. In two centuries the population would be to the means of subsistence as 256 to 9; in three centuries as 4096 to 13, and in two thousand years the difference would be almost incalculable.

In this supposition no limits whatever are placed to the produce of the earth. It may increase for ever, and be greater than any assignable quantity; yet still the power of population being in every period so much superior, the increase of the human species can only be kept down to the level of the means of subsistence by the constant operation of the strong law of necessity, acting as a check upon the greater power.

CHAPTER II.

Of the general Checks to Population, and the Mode of their Operation.

THE checks to population, which are constantly operating with more or less force in every society, and keep down the number to the level of the means of subsistence, may be classed under two general heads; the preventive and the positive checks.

The preventive check, is peculiar to man, and arises from that distinctive superiority in his reasoning faculties, which enables him to calculate distant consequences. Plants and animals have apparently no doubts about the future support of their offspring. The checks to their indefinite increase, therefore, are all positive. But man cannot look around him, and see the distress which frequently presses upon those who have large families; he cannot contemplate his present possessions or earnings, which he now nearly consumes himself, and calculate the amount of each share, when with very little addition they must be divided, perhaps, among seven or eight, without feeling a doubt, whether if he follow the bent of his inclinations, he may be able to support the offspring which he will probably bring into the world. In a state of equality, if such can exist, this would be the simple question. In the present state of society, other considerations occur. Will he not lower his rank in life, and be obliged to give up in great measure his former society? Does any mode of employment present itself by which he may reasonably hope to maintain a family? Will he not at any rate subject himself to greater difficulties, and more severe labour than in his single state? Will he not be unable to transmit to his children the same advantages of education and improvement that he had himself possessed? Does he even feel secure that, should he have a large family, his utmost exertions can save them from rags, and squalid poverty, and their consequent degradation in the community? And may he not be reduced to the grating necessity of forfeiting his independence, and of being obliged to the sparing hand of charity for support?

These considerations are calculated to prevent, and certainly do prevent, a great number of persons in all civilized nations from pursuing the dictate of nature in an early attachment to one woman.

If this restraint do not produce vice, as in many instances is the case, and very generally so among the middle and higher classes of men, it is undoubtedly the least evil that can arise from the principle of population. Considered as a restraint on an inclination, otherwise innocent, and always natural, it must be allowed to produce a certain degree of temporary unhappiness; but evidently slight, compared with the evils which result from any of the other checks to population.

When this restraint produces vice, as it does most frequently among men, and among a numerous class of females, the evils which follow are but too conspicuous. A promiscuous intercourse to such a degree as to prevent the birth of children, seems to lower in the most marked manner the dignity of human nature. It cannot be without its effect on men, and nothing can be more obvious than its tendency to degrade the female character, and to destroy all its most amiable and distinguishing characteristics. Add to which, that among those unfortunate females with which all great towns abound, more real distress and aggravated misery are, perhaps, to be found, than in any other department of human life.

When a general corruption of morals, with regard to the sex, pervades all the classes of society, its effects must necessarily be, to poison the springs of domestic happiness, to weaken conjugal and parental affection, and to lessen the united exertions and ardour of parents in the care and education of their children; effects, which cannot take place without a decided diminution of the general happiness and virtue of society; particularly, as the necessity of art in the accomplishment and conduct of intrigues, and in the concealment of their consequences, necessarily leads to many other vices.

The positive checks to population are extremely various, and include every cause, whether arising from vice or misery, which in any degree contribute to shorten the natural duration of human life. Under this head therefore may be enumerated, all unwholesome occupations, severe labour and exposure to the seasons, extreme poverty, bad nursing of children, great towns, excesses of all kinds, the whole train of common diseases and epidemics, wars, pestilence, plague, and famine.

On examining these obstacles to the increase of population which are classed under the heads of preventive and positive checks, it will appear that they are all resolvable into moral restraint, vice, and misery.

Of the preventive checks, that which is not followed by irregular gratifications, may properly be termed moral restraint.[1]

Promiscuous intercourse, unnatural passions, violations of the marriage bed, and improper arts to conceal the consequences of irregular connections, are preventive checks that clearly come under the head of vice.

Of the positive checks, those which appear to arise unavoidably from the laws of nature, may be called exclusively misery; and those which we obviously bring upon ourselves, such as wars, excesses, and many others which it would be in our power to avoid, are of a mixed nature. They are brought upon us by vice, and their consequences are misery.[a]

---

[1] [It will be observed, that I here use the term *moral* in its most confined sense. By moral restraint I would be understood to mean a restraint from marriage from prudential motives, with a conduct strictly moral during the period of this restraint; and I have never intentionally deviated from this sense. When I have wished to consider the restraint from marriage unconnected with its consequences, I have either called it prudential restraint, or a part of the preventive check, of which indeed it forms the principal branch.

In my review of the different stages of society, I have been accused of not allowing sufficient weight in the prevention of population to moral restraint; but when the confined sense of the term, which I have here explained, is adverted to, I am fearful that I shall not be found to have erred much in this respect. I should be very glad to believe myself mistaken. *Note added later.*]

[a] As the general consequence of vice is misery, and as this consequence is the precise reason why an action is termed vicious, it may appear that the term *misery* alone would be here sufficient, and that it is superfluous to

In every country, some of these checks are, with more or less force, in constant operation ; yet, notwithstanding their general prevalence, there are few states in which there is not a constant effort in the population to increase beyond the means of subsistence. This constant effort as constantly tends to subject the lower classes of society to distress, and to prevent any great permanent melioration of their condition.

These effects, in the present state of society, seem to be produced in the following manner. We will suppose the means of subsistence in any country just equal to the easy support of its inhabitants. The constant effort towards population, which is found to act even in the most vicious societies, increases the number of people before the means of subsistence are increased. The food therefore which before supported eleven millions, must now be divided among eleven millions and a half. The poor consequently must live much worse, and many of them be reduced to severe distress. The number of labourers also being above

use both. But the rejection of the term *vice* would introduce a considerable confusion into our language and ideas. We want it particularly to distinguish those actions, the general tendency of which is to produce misery, but which, in their immediate or individual effects, may produce perhaps exactly the contrary. The gratification of all our passions in its immediate effect is happiness, not misery ; and, in individual instances, even the remote consequences (at least in this life) come under the same denomination. I have little doubt that there have been some irregular connections with women, which have added to the happiness of both parties, and have injured no one. These individual actions therefore cannot come under the head of misery. But they are still evidently vicious, because an action is so denominated the general tendency of which is to produce misery, whatever may be its individual effect ; and no person can doubt the general tendency of an illicit intercourse between the sexes, to injure the happiness of society.

the proportion of work in the market, the price of labour must tend to fall; while the price of provisions would at the same time tend to rise. The labourer therefore must do more work to earn the same as he did before. During this season of distress, the discouragements to marriage, and the difficulty of rearing a family are so great, that population is nearly at a stand. In the meantime, the cheapness of labour, the plenty of labourers, and the necessity of an increased industry among them, encourage cultivators to employ more labour upon their land; to turn up fresh soil, and to manure and improve more completely what is already in tillage; till ultimately the means of subsistence may become in the same proportion to the population as at the period from which we set out. The situation of the labourer being then again tolerably comfortable, the restraints to population are in some degree loosened; and, after a short period, the same retrograde and progressive movements, with respect to happiness, are repeated.

This sort of oscillation will not probably be obvious to common view; and it may be difficult even for the most attentive observer to calculate its periods. Yet that, in the generality of old states, some such vibration does exist, though in a much less marked, and in a much more irregular manner, than I have described it, no reflecting man who considers the subject deeply can well doubt.

One principal reason why this oscillation has been less remarked, and less decidedly confirmed by experience than might naturally be expected, is, that the histories of mankind which we possess, are, in general, histories only of the higher classes. We have not many accounts, that can be

depended upon, of the manners and customs of that part
of mankind where these retrograde and progressive movements chiefly take place. A satisfactory history of this
kind, of one people and of one period, would require the
constant and minute attention of many observing minds in
local and general remarks on the state of the lower classes
of society, and the causes that influenced it; and, to draw
accurate inferences upon this subject, a succession of such
historians for some centuries would be necessary. This
branch of statistical knowledge has, of late years, been
attended to in some countries,[a] and we may promise ourselves a clearer insight into the internal structure of human
society from the progress of these inquiries. But the science may be said yet to be in its infancy, and many of the
objects, on which it would be desirable to have information,
have been either omitted or not stated with sufficient accuracy. Among these perhaps may be reckoned the proportion of the number of adults to the number of marriages;
the extent to which vicious customs have prevailed in consequence of the restraints upon matrimony; the comparative
mortality among the children of the most distressed part of
the community, and of those who live rather more at their
ease; the variations in the real price of labour; the observable differences in the state of the lower classes of society
with respect to ease and happiness, at different times during
a certain period; and very accurate registers of births,

[a] The judicious questions which Sir John Sinclair circulated in Scotland,
and the valuable accounts which he has collected in that part of the island,
do him the highest honour; and these accounts will ever remain an extraordinary monument of the learning, good sense, and general information of

deaths, and marriages, which are of the utmost importance in this subject.

A faithful history, including such particulars, would tend greatly to elucidate the manner in which the constant check upon population acts; and would probably prove the existence of the retrograde and progressive movements that have been mentioned; though the times of their vibration must necessarily be rendered irregular from the operation of many interrupting causes; such as, the introduction or failure of certain manufactures; a greater or less prevalent spirit of agricultural enterprise; years of plenty, or years of scarcity; wars, sickly seasons, poor laws, emigration, and other causes of a similar nature.

A circumstance which has perhaps more than any other contributed to conceal this oscillation from common view, is, the difference between the nominal and real price of labour. It very rarely happens that the nominal price of labour universally falls; but we well know that it frequently remains the same, while the nominal price of provisions has been gradually rising. This is, in effect, a real fall in the

the clergy of Scotland. It is to be regretted that the adjoining parishes are not put together in the work, which would have assisted the memory both in attaining and recollecting the state of particular districts. The repetitions and contradictory opinions which occur are not in my opinion so objectionable, as, to the result of such testimony, more faith may be given than we could possibly give to the testimony of any individual. Even were this result drawn for us by some master hand, though much valuable time would undoubtedly be saved, the information would not be so satisfactory. If, with a few subordinate improvements, this work had contained accurate and complete registers for the last 150 years, it would have been inestimable, and would have exhibited a better picture of the internal state of a country, than has yet been presented to the world. But this last most essential improvement no diligence could have effected.

price of labour; and, during this period, the condition of the lower classes of the community must be gradually growing worse. But the farmers and capitalists are growing rich from the real cheapness of labour. Their increasing capitals enable them to employ a greater number of men; and, as the population had probably suffered some check from the greater difficulty of supporting a family, the demand for labour, after a certain period, would be great in proportion to the supply, and its price would of course rise, if left to find its natural level; and thus the wages of labour, and consequently the condition of the lower classes of society, might have progressive and retrograde movements, though the price of labour might never nominally fall.

In savage life, where there is no regular price of labour, it is little to be doubted that similar oscillations take place. When population has increased nearly to the utmost limits of the food, all the preventive and the positive checks will naturally operate with increased force. Vicious habits with respect to the sex will be more general, the exposing of children more frequent, and both the probability and fatality, of wars and epidemicks will be considerably greater; and these causes will probably continue their operation till the population is sunk below the level of the food; and then the return to comparative plenty will again produce an increase, and, after a certain period, its further progress will again be checked by the same causes.[a]

[a] Sir James Steuart very justly compares the generative faculty to a spring loaded with a variable weight (Polit. Econ., vol. i., b. i., c. 4, p. 20) which would of course produce exactly that kind of oscillation which has been mentioned. In the first book of his Political Economy, he has explained many parts of the subject of population very ably.

But without attempting to establish in all cases these progressive and retrograde movements in different countries, which would evidently require more minute histories than we possess, the following propositions are proposed to be proved :

1. Population is necessarily limited by the means of subsistence.

2. Population invariably increases, where the means of subsistence increase, unless prevented by some very powerful and obvious checks.[1]

3. These checks, and the checks which repress the superior power of population, and keep its effects on a level with the means of subsistence, are all resolvable into moral restraint, vice, and misery.

The first of these propositions scarcely needs illustration. The second and third will be sufficiently established by a review of the immediate checks to population in the past and present state of society.

This review will be the subject of the following chapters.

[1] [I have expressed myself in this cautious manner, because I believe there are some instances where population does not keep up to the level of the means of subsistence. But these are extreme cases ; and, generally speaking, it might be said that —

1. Population is necessarily limited by the means of subsistence.

2. Population always increases where the means of subsistence increase.

3. The checks which repress the superior power of population, and keep its effects on a level with the means of subsistence, are all resolvable into moral restraint, vice, and misery.

It should be observed that, by an increase in the means of subsistence, is here meant such an increase as will enable the mass of the society to command more food. An increase might certainly take place which in the actual state of a particular society would not be distributed to the lower classes, and consequently would give no stimulus to the population. *Note added later.*]

BOOK IV.

OF OUR FUTURE PROSPECTS RESPECTING THE RE-
MOVAL OR MITIGATION OF THE EVILS ARISING
FROM THE PRINCIPLE OF POPULATION.

CHAPTER I.

*Of moral restraint, and the foundations of our obligation to practise
this virtue.*

As it appears, that in the actual state of every society
which has come within our review, the natural progress of
population has been constantly and powerfully checked; and
as it seems evident, that no improved form of government,
no plans of emigration, no benevolent institutions, and no
degree or direction of national industry, can prevent the
continued action of a great check to increase in some
form or other; it follows, that we must submit to it as an
inevitable law of nature; and the only inquiry that remains,
is, how it may take place with the least possible prejudice
to the virtue and happiness of human society. The various
checks to population, which have been observed to prevail
in the same and different countries, seem all to be resolvable into moral restraint, vice, and misery; and if our choice

be confined to these three, we cannot long hesitate in our decision respecting which it would be most eligible to encourage.

In the first edition of this essay, I observed, that, as from the laws of nature it appeared, that some check to population must exist, it was better that this check should arise from a foresight of the difficulties attending a family, and the fear of dependent poverty, than from the actual presence of want and sickness. This idea will admit of being pursued farther, and I am inclined to think, that, from the prevailing opinions respecting population, which undoubtedly originated in barbarous ages, and have been continued and circulated by that part of every community, which may be supposed to be interested in their support, we have been prevented from attending to the clear dictates of reason and nature on this subject. . . .

. . . Our obligation not to marry till we have a fair prospect of being able to support our children . . . will appear to deserve the attention of the moralist, if it can be proved, that an attention to this obligation is of more effect in the prevention of misery, than all the other virtues combined ; and that if, in violation of this duty, it were the general custom to follow the first impulse of nature and marry at the age of puberty, the universal prevalence of every known virtue in the greatest conceivable degree, would fail of rescuing society from the most wretched and desperate state of want, and all the diseases and famines which usually accompany it.

CHAPTER II.

Of the Effects which would result to Society from the general practice of this virtue.

ONE of the principal reasons, which have prevented an assent to the doctrine of the constant tendency of population to increase beyond the means of subsistence, is, a great unwillingness to believe, that the Deity would, by the laws of nature, bring beings into existence, which, by the laws of nature, could not be supported in that existence. But if, in addition to that general activity and direction of our industry put in motion by these laws, we further consider that the incidental evils arising from them, are constantly directing our attention to the proper check to population, moral restraint; and if it appear, that by a strict obedience to those duties which are pointed out to us by the light of nature and reason, and are confirmed and sanctioned by revelation, these evils may be avoided, the objection will, I trust, be removed, and all apparent imputation on the goodness of the Deity be done away.

The heathen moralists never represented happiness as attainable on earth, but through the medium of virtue ; and among their virtues, prudence ranked in the first class, and by some was even considered as including every other. The christian religion places our present as well as future happiness in the exercise of those virtues which tend to fit us for a state of superior enjoyment ; and the subjection of the passions to the guidance of reason, which, if not the whole, is a principal branch of prudence, is in consequence most particularly inculcated.

If, for the sake of illustration, we might be permitted to draw a picture of society, in which, each individual endeavoured to attain happiness by the strict fulfilment of those duties which the most enlightened of the antient philosophers deduced from the laws of nature, and which have been directly taught, and received such powerful sanctions in the moral code of Christianity, it would present a very different scene from that which we now contemplate. Every act which was prompted by the desire of immediate gratification, but which threatened an ultimate overbalance of pain, would be considered as a breach of duty ; and, consequently, no man whose earnings were only sufficient to maintain two children, would put himself in a situation in which he might have to maintain four or five, however he might be prompted to it by the passion of love. This prudential restraint, if it were generally adopted, by narrowing the supply of labour in the market, would, in the natural course of things, soon raise its price. The period of delayed gratification would be passed in saving the earnings which were above the wants of a single man, and in acquiring habits of sobriety, industry, and economy, which would enable him, in a few years, to enter into the matrimonial contract without fear of its consequences. The operation of the preventive check in this way, by constantly keeping the population within the limits of the food, though constantly following its

increase, would give a real value to the rise of wages, and
the sums saved by labourers before marriage, very different
from those forced advances in the price of labour, or arbi-
trary parochial donations, which, in proportion to their magnitude and extensiveness, must of necessity be followed by
a proportional advance in the price of provisions. As the
wages of labour would thus be sufficient to maintain with
decency a large family, and as every married couple would
set out with a sum for contingencies, all squalid poverty
would be removed from society, or, at least, be confined to
a very few, who had fallen into misfortunes against which,
no prudence or foresight could provide.

The interval between the age of puberty, and the period
at which each individual might venture on marriage, must,
according to the supposition, be passed in strict chastity ;
because the law of chastity cannot be violated without producing evil. The effect of anything like a promiscuous
intercourse, which prevents the birth of children, is evidently
to weaken the best affections of the heart, and, in a very
marked manner, to degrade the female character.. And any
other intercourse, would, without improper arts, bring as
many children into the society as marriage, with a much
greater probability of their becoming a burden to it.

These considerations show that the virtue of chastity is not,
as some have supposed, a forced produce of artificial society;
but that it has the most real and solid foundation in nature
and reason ; being apparently the only virtuous means of
avoiding the vice and misery which result so often from the
principle of population. . . .

CHAPTER X.

Of the errors in different plans which have been proposed, to improve the condition of the Poor.

. . . ARTHUR YOUNG, in most of his works, appears clearly to understand the principle of population, and is fully aware of the evils which must necessarily result from an increase of people beyond the demand for labour, and the means of comfortable subsistence. In his tour through France, he has particularly laboured this point, and shown most forcibly the misery, which results, in that country, from the excess of population occasioned by the too great division of property. Such an increase, he justly calls, merely a multiplication of wretchedness. "Couples marry and procreate on the idea, not the reality, of a maintenance; they increase beyond the demand of towns and manufactures; and the consequence is, distress, and numbers dying of diseases arising from insufficient nourishment." [a] . . .

After having once so clearly understood the principle of population as to express these and many other sentiments on the subject, equally just and important, it is not a little surprising to find Mr. Young, in a pamphlet, intitled, *The Question of Scarcity plainly stated, and Remedies considered,* (*published in* 1800,) observing that "the means which would

[a] Travels in France, vol. i. c. xii. p. 408.

of all others perhaps tend most surely to prevent future scarcities so oppressive to the poor as the present, would be to secure to every country labourer in the kingdom, that has three children and upwards, half an acre of land for potatoes, and grass enough to feed one or two cows. . . . If each had his ample potatoe ground and a cow, the price of wheat would be of little more consequence to them than it is to their brethren in Ireland."

" Every one admits the system to be good, but the question is how to enforce it."

I was by no means aware, that the excellence of the system had been so generally admitted. For myself I strongly protest against being included in the general term of *every one*, as I should consider the adoption of this system, as the most cruel and fatal blow to the happiness of the lower classes of people in this country, that they had ever received.

Mr. Young, however, goes on to say, that, " The magnitude of the object should make us disregard any difficulties, but such as are insuperable : none such would probably occur if something like the following means were resorted to :

" I. Where there are common pastures, to give to a labouring man having   children a right to demand an allotment proportioned to the family, to be set out by the parish officers, etc., . . . and a cow bought. Such labourer to have both for life, paying 40s. a year till the price of the cow, etc., was reimbursed : at his death to go to the labourer having the most numerous family, for life, paying   shillings a week to the widow of his predecessor.

" II. Labourers thus demanding allotments by reason of their families to have land assigned, and cows bought, till the proportion so allotted amounts to one   of the extent of the common.

" III. In parishes where there are no commons, and the quality of the land adequate, every cottager having children, to whose cottage there is not within a given time land sufficient for a cow, and half an acre of potatoes, assigned at a fair average rent, subject to appeal to the sessions, to have a right to demand   shillings per week of the parish for every child, till such land be assigned ; leaving to landlords and tenants the means of doing it.   Cows to be found by the parish under an annual reimbursement.

" The great object is, by means of milk and potatoes, to take the mass of the country poor from the consumption of wheat, and to give them substitutes equally wholesome and nourishing, and as independent of scarcities, natural and artificial, as the providence of the Almighty will admit."

Would not this plan operate, in the most direct manner, as an encouragement to marriage and a bounty on children, which Mr. Young has with so much justice reprobated in his travels in France? and does he seriously think that it would be an eligible thing, to feed the mass of the people in this country on milk and potatoes, and make them as independent of the price of corn, and of the demand for labour, as their brethren in Ireland?

The specifick cause of the poverty and misery of the lower classes of people in France and Ireland, is, that from the extreme subdivision of property in the one country, and the facility of obtaining a potatoe ground in the other, a population is brought into existence, which is not demanded by the quantity of capital and employment in the country ; and the consequence of which must therefore necessarily be . . . to lower in general the price of labour by too great competition ; from which must result complete indigence to those who cannot find employment, and an incomplete subsistence even to those who can.

The obvious tendency of Mr. Young's plan is, by encouraging marriage and furnishing a cheap food, independent of the price of corn, and, of course, of the demand for labour, to place the lower classes of people exactly in this situation. . . . Mr. Young's plan would be incomparably more powerful in encouraging a population beyond the demand for labour than our present poor laws. A laudable repugnance to the receiving of parish relief, arising partly from a spirit of independence not yet extinct, and partly, from the disagreeable mode in which the relief is given, undoubtedly deters many from marrying with a certainty of falling on the parish ; and the proportion of marriages to the whole population, which has before been noticed, clearly proves that the poor laws, though they have undoubtedly a considerable influence in this respect, do not encourage marriage so much as might be expected from theory. But the case would be very different, if, when a labourer had an early marriage in contemplation, the terrific forms of workhouses and parish officers, which might disturb his resolution, were to be exchanged for the fascinating visions of land and cows. If the love of property, as Mr. Young has repeatedly said, will make a man do much, it would be rather strange if it would not make him marry ; an action to which, it appears from experience, that he is by no means disinclined.

The population which would be thus called into being,

would be supported by the extended cultivation of potatoes, and would of course go on without any reference to the demand for labour. In the present state of things, notwithstanding the flourishing condition of our manufactures, and the numerous checks to our population, there is no practical problem so difficult as to find employment for the poor ; but this difficulty would evidently be aggravated a hundredfold, under the circumstances here supposed. . . .

When the commons were all divided and difficulties began to occur in procuring potatoe grounds, the habit of early marriages which had been introduced, would occasion the most complicated distress ; and when, from the increasing population and diminishing sources of subsistence, the average growth of potatoes was not more than the average consumption, a scarcity of potatoes would be in every respect, as probable, as a scarcity of wheat at present, and when it did arrive it would be beyond all comparison more dreadful.

When the common people of a country live principally upon the dearest grain, as they do in England on wheat, they have great resources in a scarcity ; and barley, oats, rice, cheap soups, and potatoes, all present themselves as less expensive, yet at the same time wholesome means of nourishment ; but when their habitual food is the lowest in this scale, they appear to be absolutely without resources, except in the bark of trees, like the poor Swedes ; and a great portion of them must necessarily be starved. . . .

The wages of labour will always be regulated by the proportion of the supply to the demand. And as, upon the potatoe system, a supply more than adequate to the demand would very soon take place, and this supply might be continued at a very cheap rate, on account of the cheapness of the food which would furnish it, the common price of labour would soon be regulated principally by the price of potatoes, instead of the price of wheat, as at present, and the rags and wretched cabins of Ireland would follow of course. . . .

Upon the same principle, it would by no means be eligible that the cheap soups of Count Rumford should be adopted as the general food of the common people. They are excellent inventions for publick institutions, and as occasional resources; but if they were once universally adopted by the poor it would be impossible to prevent the price of labour from being regulated by them; and the labourer, though at first he might have more to spare for other expenses, besides food, would ultimately have much less to spare than before. . . .

From the

APPENDIX

to the

THIRD EDITION,

1807.

———◆———

... IT has been said by some that the natural checks to population will always be sufficient to keep it within bounds without resorting to any other aids; and one ingenious writer has remarked that I have not deduced a single original fact from real observation to prove the inefficiency of the checks which already prevail.[a] These remarks are correctly true, and are truisms exactly of the same kind as the assertion that man cannot live without food. For undoubtedly as long as this continues to be a law of his nature, what are here called the natural checks cannot possibly fail of being effectual. Besides the curious truism that these assertions involve, they proceed upon the very strange supposi-

[a] I should like much to know what description of facts this gentleman had in view when he made this observation. If I could have found one of the kind which seems here to be alluded to, it would indeed have been truly original.

tion that the *ultimate* object of my work is to check population, as if anything could be more desirable than the most rapid increase of population, unaccompanied by vice and misery. But of course my ultimate object is to diminish vice and misery, and any checks to population which may have been suggested are solely as means to accomplish this end. To a rational being the prudential check to population ought to be considered as equally natural with the check from poverty and premature mortality which these gentlemen seem to think so entirely sufficient and satisfactory; and it will readily occur to the intelligent reader that one class of checks may be substituted for another, not only without essentially diminishing the population of a country, but even under a constantly progressive increase of it.[a]

On the possibility of increasing very considerably the effective population of this country, I have expressed myself in some parts of my work more sanguinely perhaps than experience would warrant. I have said that in the course of some centuries it might contain two or three times as many inhabitants as at present, and yet every person be both better fed and better clothed. And in the comparison of the increase of population and food at the beginning of the essay that the argument might not seem to depend upon a difference of opinion respecting facts, I have allowed the produce of the earth to be unlimited, which is certainly going too far. It is not a little curious therefore that it should still continue to be urged against me as an argument

[a] Both Norway and Switzerland, where the preventive check prevails the most, are increasing with some rapidity in their population; and in proportion to their means of subsistence, they can produce more males of military age than any other country of Europe.

that this country might contain two or three times as many inhabitants; and it is still more curious that some persons who have allowed the different ratios of increase on which all my principal conclusions are founded, have still asserted that no difficulty or distress could arise from population till the productions of the earth could not be further increased. I doubt whether a stronger instance could readily be produced of the total absence of the power of reasoning than this assertion after such a concession affords. It involves a greater absurdity than the saying that because a farm can by proper management be made to carry an additional stock of four head of cattle every year, that therefore no difficulty or inconvenience would arise if an additional forty were placed in it yearly.

The power of the earth to produce subsistence is certainly not unlimited, but it is strictly speaking indefinite; that is its limits are not defined, and the time will probably never arrive when we shall be able to say that no further labour or ingenuity of man could make further additions to it. But the power of obtaining an additional quantity of food from the earth by proper management and in a certain time has the most remote relation imaginable to the power of keeping pace with an unrestricted increase of population. The knowledge and industry which would enable the natives of New Holland to make the best use of the natural resources of their country must, without an absolute miracle, come to them gradually and slowly, and even then as it has amply appeared would be perfectly ineffectual as to the grand object; but the passions which prompt to the increase of population are always in full vigour, and are ready to produce their full effect even in a state of the most helpless ignorance and barbarism. It will be readily allowed that the reason why New Holland in proportion to its natural powers is not so populous as China, is the want of those human institutions which protect property and encourage industry ; but the misery and vice which prevail almost equally in both countries from the tendency of population to increase faster than the means of subsistence, form a distinct consideration and arise from a distinct cause. They arise from the incomplete discipline of the human passions, and no person with the slightest knowledge of mankind has ever had the hardihood to affirm that human institutions could completely discipline all the human passions. But I have already treated this subject so fully in the course of the work that I am ashamed to add anything further here.

The next grand objection which has been urged against me is my denial of the *right* of the poor to support.

Those who would maintain this objection with any degree of consistency are bound to show that the different ratios of increase with respect to population and food which I attempted to establish at the beginning of the essay, are fundamentally erroneous ; since on the supposition of their being true, the conclusion is inevitable. If it appear, as it must appear on these ratios being allowed, that it is not possible for the industry of man to produce on a limited territory sufficient food for all that would be born if every person were to marry at the time when he was first prompted to it by inclination, it follows irresistibly that all cannot have a *right* to support. Let us for a moment suppose an equal division of property in any country. If under these circumstances one half of the society were by prudential habits so to regulate their increase that it exactly kept pace with their increasing cultivation, it is evident that the individuals of this portion of society would always remain as rich as at first. If the other half during the same time married at the age of puberty, when they would probably feel most inclined to it, it is evident that they would soon become wretchedly poor. But upon what plea of justice or equity could this second half of the society claim a right in virtue of their poverty to any of the possessions of the first half? This poverty had arisen entirely from their own ignorance or imprudence; and it would be perfectly clear from the manner in which it had come upon them that if their plea were admitted, and they were not suffered to feel the particular evils resulting from their conduct, the whole society would shortly be involved in the same degree of wretchedness. Any voluntary and temporary assistance which might be given as a measure of charity by the richer members of the society to the others while they were learning to make a better use of the lessons of nature would be quite a distinct consideration, and without doubt most properly applied; but nothing like a claim of *right* to support can possibly be maintained till we deny the premises; till we affirm that the American increase of population is a miracle, and does not arise from the greater facility of obtaining the means of subsistence.*

a It has been said that I have written a quarto volume to prove that population increases in a geometrical and food in an arithmetical ratio, but this is not quite true. The first of these propositions I considered as proved the moment the American increase was related, and the second proposition as soon as it was enunciated. The chief object of my work

In fact whatever we may say in our declamations on this subject, almost the whole of our *conduct* is founded on the non-existence of this right. If the poor had really a claim of *right* to support, I do not think that any man could justify his wearing broadcloth or eating as much meat as he likes for dinner ; and those who assert this right, and yet are rolling in their carriages, living every day luxuriously, and keeping even their horses on food of which their fellow-creatures are in want, must be allowed to act with the greatest inconsistency. Taking an individual instance without reference to consequences, it appears to me that Mr. Godwin's argument is irresistible. Can it be pretended for a moment that a part of the mutton which I expect to eat to-day would not be much more beneficially employed on some hard-working labourer who has not perhaps tasted animal food for the last week, or on some poor family who cannot command sufficient food of any kind fully to satisfy the cravings of hunger? If these instances were not of a nature to multiply in proportion as such wants were indiscriminately gratified, the gratification of them, as it would be practicable, would be highly beneficial ; and in this case I should not have the smallest hesitation in most fully allowing the right. But as it appears clearly both from theory and experience that if

was to inquire what effects these laws, which I considered as established in the first six pages, had produced and were likely to produce on society ; a subject not very readily exhausted. The principal fault of my details is that they are not sufficiently particular ; but this was a fault which it was not in my power to remedy. It would be a most curious, and to every philosophical mind a most interesting piece of information, to know the exact share of the full power of increase which each existing check prevents ; but at present I see no mode of obtaining such information.

I

the claim were allowed it would soon increase beyond the *possibility* of satisfying it, and that the practical attempt to do so would involve the human race in the most wretched and universal poverty, it follows necessarily that our conduct which denies the right is more suited to the present state of our being than our declamations which allow it.

The great author of nature indeed with that wisdom which is apparent in all His works has not left this conclusion to the cold and speculative consideration of general consequences. By making the passion of self-love beyond comparison stronger than the passion of benevolence, He has at once impelled us to that line of conduct which is essential to the preservation of the human race. If all that might be born could be adequately supplied, we cannot doubt that He would have made the desire of giving to others as ardent as that of supplying ourselves. But since under the present constitution of things this is not so, He has enjoined every man to pursue as his primary object his own safety and happiness, and the safety and happiness of those immediately connected with him; and it is highly instructive to observe that in proportion as the sphere contracts and the power of giving effectual assistance increases, the desire increases at the same time. In the case of children who have certainly a claim of *right* to the support and protection of their parents, we generally find parental affection nearly as strong as self-love; and except in a few anomalous cases the last morsel will be divided into equal shares.

By this wise provision the most ignorant are led to promote the general happiness, an end which they would have

totally failed to attain if the moving principle of their conduct had been benevolence.[a] Benevolence indeed as the
great and constant source of action, would require the most
perfect knowledge of causes and effects, and therefore can
only be the attribute of the Deity. In a being so short-
sighted as man it would lead into the grossest errors, and
soon transform the fair and cultivated soil of civilized society
into a dreary scene of want and confusion. . . .

Among those who have objected to my declaration that the
poor have no claim of *right* to support is Mr. Young, who
with a harshness not quite becoming a candid inquirer after
truth has called my proposal for the gradual abolition of the
poor-laws a horrible plan, and asserted that the execution of
it would be a most iniquitous proceeding. Let this plan
however be compared for a moment with that which he himself and others have proposed of fixing the sum of the poor's
rates, which on no account is to be increased. Under such
a law, if the distresses of the poor were to be aggravated ten-
fold, either by the increase of numbers or the recurrence of
a scarcity, the same sum would invariably be appropriated to
their relief. If the statute which gives the poor a right to
support were to remain unexpunged, we should add to the
cruelty of starving them the injustice of still *professing* to
relieve them. If this statute were expunged or altered we
should virtually deny the right of the poor to support, and
only retain the absurdity of saying that they had a right to a

---

[a] In saying this let me not be supposed to give the slightest sanction to
the system of morals inculcated in the " Fable of the Bees," a system which
I consider as absolutely false, and directly contrary to the just definition of
virtue. The great art of Dr. Mandeville consisted in misnomers.

certain sum, an absurdity on which Mr. Young justly comments with much severity in the case of France. In both cases the hardships which they would suffer would be much more severe, and would come upon them in a much more unprepared state than upon the plan proposed in the essay.

According to this plan all that are already married, and even all that are engaged to marry during the course of the year, and all their children, would be relieved as usual; and only those who marry subsequently, and who of course may be supposed to have made better provision for contingencies, would be out of the pale of relief.

Any plan for the abolition of the poor-laws must pre-suppose a general acknowledgment that they are essentially wrong and that it is necessary to tread back our steps. With this acknowledgment, whatever objections may be made to my plan in the too frequently short-sighted views of policy, I have no fear of comparing it with any other that has yet been advanced in point of justice and humanity; and of course the terms iniquitous and horrible " pass by me like the idle wind which I regard not."

Mr. Young it would appear has now given up this plan. He has pleaded for the privilege of being inconsistent, and has given such reasons for it that I am disposed to acquiesce in them. . . .

Mr. Young objects very strongly to that passage of the essay in which I observe that a man who plunges himself into poverty and dependence by marrying without any prospect of being able to maintain his family, has more reason to accuse himself than the price of labour, the parish, the avarice of the rich, the institutions of society, and the dispensations of Providence ; except as far as he has been deceived by those who ought to have instructed him. In answer to this, Mr. Young says that the poor fellow is justified in every one of these complaints, that of Providence alone excepted ; and that seeing other cottagers living comfortably with three or four acres of land, he has cause to accuse institutions which deny him that which the rich could well spare, and which would give him all he wants.[a] I would beg Mr. Young for a moment to consider how the matter would stand if his own plan were completely executed. After all the commons had been divided as he has proposed, if a labourer had more than one son, in what respect would the second or third be in a different situation from the man that I have supposed ? Mr. Young cannot posssibly mean to say that if he had the very natural desire of marrying at twenty, he would still have a right to complain that the society did not give him a house and three or four acres of land. . . .

To much of Mr. Young's plan as he has at present explained it I should by no means object. The peculiar evil which I apprehended from it, that of taking the poor from the consumption of wheat and feeding them on milk and potatoes, might certainly be avoided by a limitation of the number of cottages ; and I entirely agree with him in thinking that we should not be deterred from making 500,000 families more comfortable because we cannot extend the same relief to all the rest. I have indeed myself ventured to recommend a general improvement of cottages, and even the cow system on a limited scale ; and perhaps, with proper

[a] Annals of Agriculture, No. 239, p. 226.

precautions, a certain portion of land might be given to a considerable body of the labouring classes.

If the law which entitles the poor to support were to be repealed, I should most highly approve of any plan which would tend to render such repeal more palatable on its first promulgation ; and in this view some kind of compact with the poor might be very desirable. A plan of letting land to labourers under certain conditions has lately been tried in the parish of Long Newnton, in Gloucestershire ; and the result with a general proposal founded on it has been submitted to the public by Mr. Estcourt. The present success has been very striking ; but in this and every other case of the kind we should always bear in mind that no experiment respecting a provision for the poor can be said to be complete till succeeding generations have arisen.[a] I doubt if ever there has been an instance of anything like a liberal institution for the poor which did not succeed on its first establishment, however it might have failed afterwards. But this consideration should by no means deter us from making such experiments when present good is to be obtained by them, and a future overbalance of evil is not justly to be apprehended. It should only make us less rash in drawing our inferences.

With regard to the general question of the advantages to

[a] In any plan, particularly of a distribution of land as a compensation for the relief given by the poor laws, the succeeding generations would form the grand difficulty. All others would be perfectly trivial in comparison. For a time everything might go on very smoothly and the rates be much diminished ; but afterwards they would either increase again as rapidly as before or the scheme would be exposed to all the same objections which have been made to mine, without the same justice and consistency to palliate them.

the lower classes of possessing land, it should be recollected that such possessions are by no means a novelty. Formerly this system prevailed in almost every country with which we are acquainted, and prevails at present in many countries where the peasants are far from being remarkable for their comforts, but are on the contrary very poor and particularly subject to scarcities. With respect to this latter evil indeed it is quite obvious that a peasantry which depends principally on its possessions in land must be more exposed to it than one which depends on the general wages of labour. When a year of deficient crops occurs in a country of any extent and diversity of soil, it is always partial, and some districts are more affected than others. But when a bad crop of grass, corn, or potatoes, or a mortality among cattle, falls on a poor man whose principal dependence is on two or three acres of land, he is in the most deplorable and helpless situation. He is comparatively without money to purchase supplies, and is not for a moment to be compared with the man who depends on the wages of labour, and who will of course be able to purchase that portion of the general crop, whatever it may be, to which his relative situation in the society entitles him. In Sweden, where the farmers' labourers are paid principally in land and often keep two or three cows, it is not uncommon for the peasants of one district to be almost starving while their neighbours at a little distance are living in comparative plenty. It will be found indeed generally that in almost all the countries which are particularly subject to scarcities and famines, either the farms are very small or the labourers are paid principally in land. China, Indostan, and the former state of the Highlands of Scotland, furnish some proofs among many others of the truth of this observation; and in reference to the small properties of France, Mr. Young himself in his Tour particularly notices the distress arising from the least failure of the crops, and observes that such a deficiency as in England passes almost without notice, in France is attended with dreadful calamities.[a]

Should any plan therefore of assisting the poor by land be adopted in this country, it would be absolutely essential to its ultimate success to prevent them from making it their principal dependence. And this might probably be done by attending strictly to the two following rules. Not to let the division of land be so great as to interrupt the cottager essentially in his usual labours; and always to stop in the further distribution of land and cottages when the price of labour, independently of any assistance from land, would not at the average price of corn maintain three or at least two children. Could the matter be so ordered that the labourer in working for others should still continue to earn the same real command over the necessaries of life that he did before, a very great accession of comfort and happiness might accrue to the poor from the possession of land without any evil that I can foresee at present. But if these points were not attended to, I should certainly fear an approximation to the state of the poor in France, Sweden, and Ireland; nor do I think that any of the partial experiments that have yet taken place afford the slightest presumption to the contrary. The

[a] Travels in France, vol. i. c. xii. p. 409. That country will probably be the least liable to scarcities in which agriculture is carried on as the most flourishing *manufacture* of the state.

result of these experiments is indeed exactly such as one should have expected. Who could ever have doubted that if without lowering the price of labour, or taking the labourer off from his usual occupations, you could give him the produce of one or two acres of land and the benefit of a cow, you would decidedly raise his condition? But it by no means follows that he would retain this advantage if the system were so extended as to make the land his principal dependence, to lower the price of labour, and in the language of Mr. Young, to take the poor from the consumption of wheat and feed them on milk and potatoes. It does not appear to me so marvellous as it does to Mr. Young that the very same system, which in Lincolnshire and Rutlandshire may produce now the most comfortable peasantry in the British dominions, should in the end if extended without proper precautions assimilate the condition of the labourers of this country to that of the lower classes of the Irish. . . .

There is only one subject more which I shall notice, and that is rather a matter of feeling than of argument. Many persons whose understandings are not so constituted that they can regulate their belief or disbelief by their likes or dislikes, have professed their perfect conviction of the truth of the general principles contained in the essay, but at the same time have lamented this conviction as throwing a darker shade over our views of human nature, and tending particularly to narrow our prospects of future improvement. In these feelings I cannot agree with them. If from a review of the past I could not only believe that a fundamental and very extraordinary improvement in human society was possible, but feel a firm confidence that it would take place,

I should undoubtedly be grieved to find that I had over-looked some cause the operation of which would at once blast my hopes. But if the contemplation of the past history of mankind, from which alone we can judge of the future, renders it almost impossible to feel such confidence, I confess that I had much rather believe that some real and deeply-seated difficulty existed, the constant struggle with which was calculated to rouse the natural inactivity of man, to call forth his faculties, and invigorate and improve his mind, — a species of difficulty which it must be allowed is most eminently and peculiarly suited to a state of probation, than that nearly all the evils of life might with the most perfect facility be removed but for the perverseness and wicked-ness of those who influence human institutions.[a]

A person who held this latter opinion must necessarily live in a constant state of irritation and disappointment. The ardent expectations with which he might begin life would soon receive the most cruel check. The regular progress of society under the most favourable circumstances, would to him appear slow and unsatisfactory; but instead even of this regular progress his eye would be more frequently presented with retrograde movements and the most disheartening reverses. The changes to which he had looked forward with delight would be found big with new

---

[a] The misery and vice arising from the pressure of the population too hard against the limits of subsistence, and the misery and vice arising from promiscuous intercourse, may be considered as the Scylla and Charybdis of human life. That it is possible for each individual to steer clear of both these rocks is certainly true, and a truth which I have endeavoured strongly to maintain; but that these rocks do not form a difficulty independent of human institutions no person with any knowledge of the subject can venture to assert.

and unlooked-for evils, and the characters on which he had reposed the most confidence would be seen frequently deserting his favourite cause, either from the lessons of experience or the temptations of wealth and power. In this state of constant disappointment he would be but too apt to attribute everything to the worst motives, he would be inclined to give up the cause of improvement in despair, and judging of the whole from a part, nothing but a peculiar goodness of heart and amiableness of disposition could preserve him from that sickly and disgusting misanthropy which is but too frequently the end of such characters.

On the contrary, a person who held the other opinion, as he would set out with more moderate expectations, would of course be less liable to disappointment. A comparison of the best with the worst states of society, and the obvious inference from analogy that the best were capable of further improvement, would constantly present to his mind a prospect sufficiently animating to warrant his most persevering exertions. But aware of the difficulties with which the subject was surrounded, knowing how often in the attempt to attain one object some other had been lost, and that though society had made rapid advances in some directions it had been comparatively stationary in others, he would be constantly prepared for failures. These failures instead of creating despair would only create knowledge, instead of checking his ardour would give it a wiser and more successful direction, and having founded his opinion of mankind on broad and general grounds, the disappointment of any particular views would not change this opinion; but even in declining age he would probably be found believing as firmly in the reality and general prevalence of virtue as in the existence and frequency of vice, and to the last looking forward with a just confidence to those improvements in society which the history of the past, in spite of all the reverses with which it is accompanied, seems clearly to warrant.

It may be true that if ignorance is bliss 'tis folly to be wise ; but if ignorance be not bliss, as in the present instance, if all false views of society must not only impede decidedly the progress of improvement, but necessarily terminate in the most bitter disappointments to the individuals who formed them, I shall always think that the feelings and prospects of those who make the justest estimates of our future expectations are the most consolatory, and that the characters of this description are happier themselves, at the same time that they are beyond comparison more likely to contribute to the improvement and happiness of society.

From the

PREFACE

to the

FIFTH EDITION,

1817.

———◆◇◆———

THIS essay was first published at a period of extensive warfare, combined, from peculiar circumstances, with a most prosperous foreign commerce.

It came before the public, therefore, at a time when there would be an extraordinary demand for men, and very little disposition to suppose the possibility of any evil arising from the redundancy of population. Its success under these disadvantages was greater than could have been reasonably expected ; and it may be presumed that it will not lose its interest, after a period of a different description has succeeded, which has in the most marked manner illustrated its principles and confirmed its conclusions. . . .

EAST INDIA COLLEGE, *June* 7, 1817.

From the

APPENDIX

to the

FIFTH EDITION,

1817.

———◦✦◦———

Since the publication of the last edition of this essay in 1807 two works have appeared, the avowed objects of which are directly to oppose its principles and conclusions. These are " The Principles of Population and Production," by Mr. Weyland; and " An Inquiry into the Principle of Population," by Mr. James Grahame.

I would willingly leave the question as it at present stands to the judgment of the public without any attempt on my part to influence it further by a more particular reply; but as I professed my readiness to enter into the discussion of any serious objections to my principles and conclusions which were brought forward in a spirit of candour and truth, and as one at least of the publications above mentioned may be so characterized, and the other is by no means deficient in personal respect, I am induced shortly to notice them. . . .

Mr. Grahame in his second chapter, speaking of the tendency exhibited by the law of human increase to a redundancy of population, observes that some philosophers have considered this tendency as a mark of the foresight of nature, which has thus provided a ready supply for the waste of life occasioned by human vices and passions; while "others, of whom Mr. Malthus is the leader, regard the vices and follies of human nature and their various products, famine, disease, and war, as *benevolent remedies* by which nature has enabled human beings to correct the disorders that would arise from that redundance of population which the unrestrained operation of her laws would create."[1]

These are the opinions imputed to me and the philosophers with whom I am associated. If the imputation were just, we have certainly on many accounts great reason to be ashamed of ourselves. For what are we made to say? In the first place, we are stated to assert that famine is a benevolent remedy for *want of food*, as redundance of population admits of no other interpretation than that of a people ill supplied with the means of subsistence, and consequently the benevolent remedy of famine here noticed can only apply to the disorders arising from scarcity of food.

Secondly, We are said to affirm that nature enables human beings by means of diseases to correct the disorders that would arise from a redundance of population — that is, that mankind willingly and purposely create diseases with a view to prevent those diseases which are the necessary conse-

[1] P. 100.

quences of a redundant population, and are not worse or more mortal than the means of prevention.

And thirdly, it is imputed to us generally that we consider the vices and follies of mankind as benevolent remedies for the disorders arising from a redundant population, and it follows as a matter of course that these vices ought to be encouraged rather than reprobated.

It would not be easy to compress in so small a compass a greater quantity of absurdity, inconsistency, and unfounded assertion.

The two first imputations may perhaps be peculiar to Mr. Grahame, and protection from them may be found in their gross absurdity and inconsistency. With regard to the third it must be allowed that it has not the merit of novelty. Although it is scarcely less absurd than the two others, and has been shown to be an opinion nowhere to be found in the essay nor legitimately to be inferred from any part of it, it has been continually repeated in various quarters for fourteen years, and now appears in the pages of Mr. Grahame. For the last time I will now notice it, and should it still continue to be brought forward I think I may be fairly excused from paying the slightest further attention either to the imputation itself or to those who advance it.

If I had merely stated that the tendency of the human race to increase faster than the means of subsistence was kept to a level with these means by some or other of the forms of vice and misery, and that these evils were absolutely unavoidable and incapable of being diminished by any human efforts, still I could not with any semblance of justice be accused of considering vice and misery as the remedies of these evils instead of the very evils themselves. As well nearly might I be open to Mr. Grahame's imputations of considering the famine and disease necessarily arising from a scarcity of food as a benevolent remedy for the evils which this scarcity occasions.

But I have not so stated the proposition. I have not considered the evils of vice and misery arising from a redundant population as unavoidable and incapable of being diminished. On the contrary, I have pointed out a mode by which these evils may be removed or mitigated by removing or mitigating their cause. I have endeavoured to show that this may be done consistently with human virtue and happiness. I have never considered any possible increase of population as an evil, except as far as it might increase the proportion of vice and misery. Vice and misery, and these alone, are the evils which it has been my great object to contend against. I have expressly proposed moral restraint as their rational and proper remedy; and whether the remedy be good or bad, adequate or inadequate, the proposal itself and the stress which I have laid upon it is an incontrovertible proof that I never can have considered vice and misery as themselves remedies.

But not only does the general tenour of my work and the specific object of the latter part of it clearly show that I do not consider vice and misery as remedies, but particular passages in various parts of it are so distinct on the subject as not to admit of being misunderstood by the most perverse blindness.

It is therefore quite inconceivable that any writer with the slightest pretensions to respectability should venture to bring

K

forward such imputations, and it must be allowed to show
either such a degree of ignorance or such a total want of
candour as utterly to disqualify him for the discussion of
such subjects.

But Mr. Grahame's misrepresentations are not confined
to the passage above referred to. In his introduction he
observes that in order to check a redundant population, the
evils of which I consider as much nearer than Mr. Wallace,
I "recommend immediate recourse to human efforts to the
restraint prescribed by Condorcet for the correction or mitigation of the evil." This is an assertion entirely without
foundation. I have never adverted to the check suggested
by Condorcet without the most marked disapprobation.
Indeed I should always particularly reprobate any artificial
and unnatural modes of checking population, both on
account of their immorality and their tendency to remove
a necessary stimulus to industry. If it were possible for
each married couple to limit by a wish the number of their
children, there is certainly reason to fear that the indolence
of the human race would be very greatly increased, and
that neither the population of individual countries nor of
the whole earth would ever reach its natural and proper
extent. But the restraints which I have recommended are
quite of a different character. They are not only pointed
out by reason and sanctioned by religion, but tend in the
most marked manner to stimulate industry. It is not easy
to conceive a more powerful encouragement to exertion and
good conduct than the looking forward to marriage as a
state peculiarly desirable : but only to be enjoyed in comfort by the acquisition of habits of industry, economy, and

prudence. And it is in this light that I have always wished to place it. . . .

With regard to the substance and aim of Mr. Grahame's work, it seems to be intended to show that emigration is the remedy provided by nature for a redundant population, and that if this remedy cannot be adequately applied there is no other that can be proposed which will not lead to consequences worse than the evil itself. These are two points which I have considered at length in the essay, and it cannot be necessary to repeat any of the arguments here. Emigration, if it could be freely used, has been shown to be a resource which could not be of long duration. It cannot therefore under any circumstances be considered as an adequate remedy. The latter position is a matter of opinion, and may rationally be held by any person who sees reason to think it well founded. It appears to me, I confess, that experience most decidedly contradicts it, but to those who think otherwise there is nothing more to be said than that they are bound in consistency to acquiesce in the necessary consequences of their opinion. These consequences are that the poverty and wretchedness arising from a redundant population, or in other words from very low wages and want of employment, are absolutely irremediable and must be continually increasing as the population of the earth proceeds ; and that all the efforts of legislative wisdom and private charity, though they may afford a wholesome and beneficial exercise of human virtue and may occasionally alter the distribution and vary the pressure of human misery, can do absolutely nothing towards diminishing the general amount or checking the increasing weight of this pressure. . . .

It was my object in the two chapters on *Moral Restraint*, and its *Effects on Society*, to show that the evils arising from the principle of population were exactly of the same nature as the evils arising from the excessive or irregular gratification of the human passions in general, and that from the existence of these evils we had no more reason to conclude that the principle of increase was too strong for the purpose intended by the Creator, than to infer from the existence of the vices arising from the human passions that these passions required diminution or extinction, instead of regulation and direction.

If this view of the subject be allowed to be correct, it will naturally follow that notwithstanding the acknowledged evils occasioned by the principle of population, the advantages derived from it under the present constitution of things may very greatly overbalance them.

A slight sketch of the nature of these advantages as far as the main object of the essay would allow was given in the two chapters to which I have alluded ; but the subject has lately been pursued with great ability in the work of Mr. Sumner on the "Records of the Creation ; " and I am happy to refer to it as containing a masterly development and completion of views of which only an intimation could be given in the essay.

I fully agree with Mr. Sumner as to the beneficial effects which result from the principle of population, and feel entirely convinced that the natural tendency of the human race to increase faster than the possible increase of the means of subsistence could not be either destroyed or essentially diminished without diminishing that hope of rising and fear of falling in society so necessary to the improvement of the human faculties and the advancement of human happiness. But with this conviction on my mind, I feel no wish to alter the view which I have given of the evils arising from the principle of population. These evils do not lose their name or nature because they are overbalanced by good, and to consider them in a different light on this account and cease to call them evils would be as irrational as the objecting to call the irregular indulgences of passion vicious, and to affirm that they lead to misery because our passions are the main sources of human virtue and happiness.

I have always considered the principle of population as a law peculiarly suited to a state of discipline and trial. Indeed I believe that, in the whole range of the laws of nature with which we are acquainted, not one can be pointed out which in so remarkable a manner tends to strengthen and confirm this scriptural view of the state of man on earth. And as each individual has the power of avoiding the evil consequences to himself and society resulting from the principle of population by the practice of a virtue clearly dictated to him by the light of nature, and sanctioned by revealed religion, it must be allowed that the ways of God to man with regard to this great law of nature are completely vindicated.

I have therefore certainly felt surprise as well as regret that no inconsiderable part of the objections which have been made to the principles and conclusions of the " Essay on Population " has come from persons for whose moral and religious character I have so high a respect that it would have been particularly gratifying to me to obtain their approbation and sanction. This effect has been attributed to some expressions used in the course of the work which have been thought too harsh, and not sufficiently indulgent to the weakness of human nature and the feelings of Christian charity.

It is probable that having found the bow bent too much one way I was induced to bend it too much the other in order to make it straight. But I shall always be quite ready to blot out any part of the work which is considered by a competent tribunal as having a tendency to prevent the bow from becoming finally straight and to impede the progress of truth. In deference to this tribunal I have already expunged the passages which have been most objected to, and I have made some few further corrections of the same kind in the present edition. By these alterations I hope and believe that the work has been improved without impairing its principles. But I still trust that whether it is read with or without these alterations, every reader of candour must acknowledge that the practical design uppermost in the mind of the writer, with whatever want of judgment it may have been executed, is to improve the condition and increase the happiness of the lower classes of society.

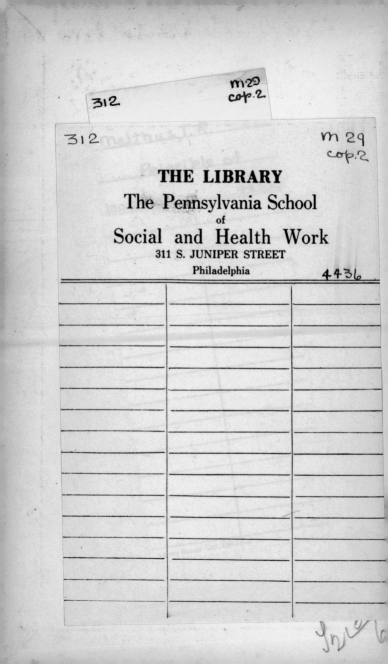